THE
STAFFORDS

Portrait of Lord and Lady Stafford.

THE
STAFFORDS

John Martin Robinson

Phillimore

2002

Published by
PHILLIMORE & CO. LTD
Shopwyke Manor Barn, Chichester, West Sussex, England

ISBN 1 86077 219 6

Printed and bound in Great Britain by
BUTLER AND TANNER LTD
London and Frome

Contents

❦

Foreword by Lord Stafford vii

Preface xi

   I   INTRODUCTION: The Origins of the Stafford Family
      and Stafford Castle 1066-1300 1

   II   Earls and Bishops 7

  III   The Dukes of Buckingham 19

  IV   The Tragedy of the Third Duke 35

   V   From Dukes to Shoemakers 49

  VI   Viscount Stafford and the Earls of Stafford 67

 VII   The Jerninghams 79

VIII   Revival of the Stafford Peerage 97

  IX   Mrs Fitzherbert 111

POSTSCRIPT: The Fitzherberts 125

PEDIGREES: Early Staffords and Dukes of Buckingham 128
                Stafford Howards 129
                The Fitzherberts of Norbury 129
                Stafford Jerningham and Fitzherbert 130

Notes 131

Select Bibliography 135

Index 141

Foreword by Lord Stafford

৩৯·৫৫৫

I COMMISSIONED THIS BOOK to trace and illuminate the complicated descent of the Stafford barony through several different families before it came to the Fitzherberts at the beginning of the 20th century. The Fitzherberts have now held the title slightly longer than the Stafford Jerninghams, our immediate predecessors in the title. This book is not a history of the Fitzherberts of Norbury, my direct male line ancestors, but of my collateral forebears, the successive Lords Stafford.

To set the context, however, it might be helpful if I said a few words about the Fitzherberts who are of considerable interest in their own right as a family of medieval descent who had particularly turbulent and interesting lives during the 16th-century Reformation.

As well as being the 15th Lord Stafford, I am also the 29th Lord of the Manor of Norbury in Derbyshire, the Fitzherberts of Swynnerton, my immediate family, having succeeded as heads of the family on the death of their cousin Sir John Fitzherbert of Norbury, a colonel of dragoons in the Royalist army, in 1649. Since then Swynnerton Hall in Staffordshire has been the family seat rather than the old manor house at Norbury, though we owned the latter until 1881 and I still hold the Lordship of the Manor today.

The Manor of Norbury in Dovedale, Derbyshire, was originally granted to William Fitzherbert in 1125 by the Prior of Tutbury. Remarkably, the original deed (witnessed by Henry de Ferrers, Earl of Derby) survives in my possession. From 1125 the manor has passed in unbroken male descent to the present generation, unlike the Stafford descent which passed several times through female heiresses before it reached the Fitzherberts in 1913. The medieval church at Norbury, which was rebuilt by the family, retains a splendid array of stone and alabaster Fitzherbert tombs, and heraldic glass, while the old stone manor house adjoining now belongs to the National Trust.

From the 13th to the 15th centuries the Fitzherberts were prominent locally in Derbyshire and Nottinghamshire, Knights of the shire and frequently serving as sheriff. But it was their 16th-century standing and experience which made them so interesting. Their story as loyal Catholics during the upheavals of the Tudor Reformation is particularly remarkable, even among the stirring tales of the English recusants, and they were also prominent in the fields of agriculture, the Law and books.

John Fitzherbert, 13th Lord of the Manor of Norbury, who was born in 1450 and died in 1531 aged 81, is best known as an agricultural pioneer, farming at Norbury for 58 years and being at the forefront of the Tudor 'agriculture revolution'. He enclosed much land for sheep farming (wool being England's most valuable export) and wrote two practical guides: *The Book of Surveying* and *The Boke of Husbandry*, the latter being published in 1523. (There is a first edition in the British Library.) He died peacefully in his bed one year before Thomas Cranmer became Archbishop of Canterbury. Cranmer's solution of 'The King's Great Matter', Henry VIII's divorce from Catherine of Aragon, ignited the English Reformation. Three generations of the family were caught up in the ensuing crisis, several of them dying in prison for their principles: a remarkable demonstration of integrity.

Sir Anthony (1470-1538), the youngest brother and successor of John 'the Agriculturalist', was a distinguished lawyer who became a Justice of the Common Bench (the equivalent of a modern High Court judge) and published the last part of *La Grande Abridgement of the Common Law* in 1516, an important codification of the Common Law. The great religious changes of the time, and the moral dilemmas associated with them, created unusual difficulties for him, like all those in authority under Henry VIII. He survived. While serving the King on several special legal commissions, including the trials of Sir Thomas More and Queen Anne Boleyn, he distanced himself from radical religious change and on his deathbed in 1538 advised his children never to accept confiscated church land.

His son, Sir Thomas (1517-1591), saw the family reach its widest extent of territorial wealth, he being the third generation of Fitzherberts to marry a rich heiress, but all the promise to which he was born was blighted by the contemporary religious troubles and his unswerving beliefs. He was described in a letter to Lord Burghley, Queen Elizabeth's minister, as a 'very stiff man'. He was arrested in 1561, at the age of 44 and imprisoned in the Fleet Prison in London. For the next thirty years he was dragged from prison to prison and finally died in the Tower in 1591.

Thomas' younger brother John, who lived at Padley in Derbyshire, was fined the huge sum of £10,000 for harbouring Catholic priests; and two such, Nichols Garlick and Robert Ludlam (who were found hiding at his house) were executed at Derby in 1588 when the Spanish Armada made all Catholic adherence seem close to High Treason. John of Padley's eldest son Thomas ignobly helped to betray his father, and plotted against his uncle in the hope of speeding up his inheritance. He is known to posterity as 'the Traitor'.

Other members of the family remained true Catholics. Nicholas, the younger brother of 'the Traitor', after studying at Exeter College Oxford, went into exile in Italy and became secretary to Cardinal Allen, the Lancashire-born leader of the English counter-Reformation and founder of the English College at Douai. He is buried in Florence. His cousin Thomas (1552-1640), who was also educated at Oxford, became a Jesuit priest after the death of his wife, wrote several books, of which *Policy and Religion* published in 1615 was the most notable – and from 1618 to a year before his death in 1640 was Rector of the English College in Rome.

The last of the senior line of the Fitzherberts of Norbury, Sir John (1604-1649), 'the Colonel', was the nephew of Nicholas 'the Jesuit'. He spent much of the depleted family fortune raising troops for the King in the Civil War and died at Lichfield in 1649 deeply in debt.

Once the Fitzherberts of Swynnerton had succeeded as heads of the family, through the 18th and 19th centuries, successive generations performed a tranquil role as Staffordshire landowners and country squires, though a more high-profile note was introduced by the widow of Thomas Fitzherbert, Maria (Smythe) Fitzherbert, who subsequently became the wife of the Prince Regent. Her connection with both the Fitzherberts and the Stafford Jerninghams (as a result of the marriage of her adopted daughter, Marianne), means that she plays a part in the story of the Stafford descent and therefore stars in the main text of this book, which I commend to the reader as illustrating a long sweep of English social and religious history, and which forms an interesting part of our national jigsaw.

FRANCIS STAFFORD
August 2002

Preface

❧ · ❧

Tᴴᴱ ʜɪsᴛᴏʀʏ ᴏꜰ ᴛʜᴇ Sᴛᴀꜰꜰᴏʀᴅs is not just the story of one family but of five successive families: the Norman de Toenis, the Bagots, a cadet line of the Howards, the Jerninghams and finally the Fitzherberts, through whom the Stafford descent has wandered via female heiresses over nine centuries. Few English titles and family descents are so complicated. Each of these five families would be worth a history in their own right and some of them have already been much published, but that is not the purpose of the present book, which is primarily to trace the story of the successive holders of the Stafford lordship in a lucid and intelligible manner. For the sake of clarity, long detours into other great families into which the Staffords married have been avoided, as has the pre-history of the successive families before they acceded to the title.

Through all the vicissitudes of descent there has been a single constant, namely, the ownership of Stafford Castle from its construction in the 11th century by the de Toenis after the Norman Conquest, down to Francis Fitzherbert of Swynnerston, 15th Lord Stafford who owns it today. The ownership of the castle at various dates has supported the revival of the title in different lines, notably Henry Stafford's claim in 1547, the Howards' in the 17th century, and the Jerninghams' in the early 19th century.

Before plunging into the details of this long family history it is necessary to outline the bare bones of the plot to prevent the reader getting lost in the minutiae of successive lords, earls, dukes, lords, viscounts, earls, and finally lords again. The story falls into two halves, the break occurring in the reign of Henry VIII, in 1521. The medieval history of the Staffords is that of the seemingly inexorable rise of a family of Anglo-Norman origin to great magnate status: the Staffords in four hundred years achieved social and economic pre-eminence under the Crown in England, becoming premier dukes as well as the owner of huge estates stretching across 24 different counties as well as the Marches of Wales. This expansion upwards and outwards from their original base in Staffordshire was the result of a series of marriages to great heiresses, and of successful careers in the King's Wars especially in the Hundred Years War against France with its unequalled opportunities for enrichment and advancement. The history of the Staffords in the medieval period reflects national history, seen from the top of the tree.

The second half of the story is quite different, for the successive families who inherited the Stafford barony, though noble and sometimes decently prosperous, were not in the mainstream and to some extent were a persecuted minority. They were all recusant Catholics who steadfastly refused to conform to the Established Church but clung to the 'Old Faith' of which they were as proud as they were of their grand medieval ancestry. Many 17th- and 18th-century daughters of the family became nuns abroad. One head of the family was beheaded and is numbered among the beatified English Catholic martyrs. This makes the later history of the Staffords different from that of most other English aristocratic lines, and is particularly interesting for that reason. Their religious allegiance gives a coherence and unity to the later descent of the title through three different but inter-related families.

The medieval English peerage was not a caste of ancient blood made up of a fixed group of noble families. On the contrary, it fluctuated over the centuries principally as a result of the failure of male heirs (caused by infertility, disease, war and civil violence) and their frequent replacement by new recruits who had married heiresses. In the later Middle Ages the ranks of the great magnates – the earls and dukes – were particularly unstable. Men who rose within the peerage and gained new or revived titles owed their success to military or administrative service to the Crown, their relationship to the King and to inheritances from other families through marriage to heiresses. The ascent of the Stafford family in the 14th and 15th centuries, from a simple barony through multiple earldoms to a dukedom and the head of the English peerage, reflects all these factors, and makes a gripping story of success interspersed with tragedies and disasters, but nothing absolutely fatal until 1521, when the dukedom and earldoms were lost. The barony, however, was revived again and again and again, and has continued into the 21st century.

The Staffords traced their ancestry back to Robert de Toeni, a Norman who followed William the Conqueror to England and built Stafford Castle. The Toeni Stafford family, however, died out in the male line leaving an heiress who married Hervey Bagot. Their descendants, having inherited Stafford Castle and its lands, also took Stafford as their surname. They married other heiresses and served in the Welsh and Scottish Wars of Edward I and Edward II. They did not reach the first rank of the nobility until the reign of Edward III when they were created Earls of Stafford. Between the creation of the earldom in 1351 and the final attainder of the dukedom in 1521, five holders of the titles, or their heirs, met violent ends (while three others died prematurely), but they never lacked a successor in the male line. This was thanks to their unusual record of fertility for a medieval noble family. Despite dramatic bouleversements, therefore, they persisted and absorbed the land holdings of other families less successful than themselves at providing heirs.

Ralph, the 1st Earl of Stafford owed his title to a long career of civil and military service to Edward III, especially in the Hundred Years War where he played a key role in the conquest of Brittany and fought at Crecy, with the Black Prince. In 1348 he was one of the Founder Knights of the Garter. His profits from the War were substantial, but his major coup was the abduction and marriage of a great heiress Margaret Audley, who brought him large estates including Tonbridge in Kent and Thornbury in Gloucestershire, to add to his ancestral lands in Staffordshire. As well as these important new castles in other parts of the country, Ralph rebuilt Stafford Castle in a smart French-influenced manner, parts of which survive today.

Ralph's second son and heir, Hugh, also gained distinction in the French Wars. He, too, was made a Knight of the Garter, and he served as a councillor to Richard II. He died on the return journey from a pilgrimage to the Holy Land. He had five sons, but several died young. The eldest was murdered before inheriting and the title passed rapidly through three younger sons who all died prematurely. Edmund, the 5th Earl of Stafford, however, made the greatest of all the family's grand marriage alliances. His wife Anne was heiress through her mother to half the Bohun estates, the Earldom of Buckingham, and to one of the Great Offices of State: The Lord High Constable of England, as well as a royal descent from Edward III. As a result of this staggering but complicated inheritance, their son Humphry Stafford found himself one of the richest men in England, and on the strength of this he was raised to a dukedom as 1st Duke of Buckingham. He played an important role in the complicated politics of the mid-15th century when the personal rule of Henry VI collapsed into chaos and Civil War. He was killed at the Battle of Northampton in 1461 fighting on the Lancastrian side. He was succeeded by his grandson Henry whose mother Margaret Beaufort was the first cousin of Henry VII's mother, also Margaret Beaufort, giving the Stafford family a splendid but fatal double descent from the Plantagenet kings.

The 2nd Duke of Buckingham played a key role in Richard III's usurpation of the throne in 1483, and at Richard's coronation, but almost immediately afterwards turned against his former ally and led an abortive revolt from Wales against Richard. This failed and he was captured and executed. His little son Edward was hidden and protected by the duke's retainers and after the victory of Henry VII at Bosworth was restored as 3rd Duke of Buckingham and brought up in the Royal Household. Duke Edward was the richest and grandest of all the Staffords, the premier duke and largest landowner in England. Though his rent roll was theoretically enormous, he never received his full income. The impoverished Welsh Marcher estates, in particular, proved intractable, ungovernable and unexploitable; his attempts to raise money and tighten up the administration merely provoked unrest and trouble, alienating his tenants and servants. The Tudors distrusted the great magnates, especially those like the Staffords of royal descent, as possible threats to the Crown. In 1521 the duke was suddenly arrested, tried for high treason, condemned on the evidence of three disgruntled retainers, and executed on Tower Hill. All the titles were attainted and the estates confiscated by Henry VIII.

This dramatic fall marked a watershed in the history of the family which was never to attain such pre-eminence and wealth again. The 3rd Duke's son Henry was well-educated and scholarly. He received Stafford Castle and in due course a few other family estates including Thornbury (his father's incomplete house in Gloucestershire) and was re-created Baron Stafford in 1547. This new title descended in his family through the remainder of the 16th century. The Staffords continued to live at Stafford Castle despite increasing financial difficulties. The 3rd Lord Stafford (of the new creation) entertained Queen Elizabeth I at the castle in 1575. On the death of Henry 5th Lord Stafford as a 16-year-old minor and ward of the Earl of Arundel in 1637, his sister Mary was married to Lord Arundel's youngest son William Howard. Though there was a male Stafford heir, Roger, he was unmarried and living in obscure circumstances in Shropshire. His sister's son was a shoemaker. Charles I, therefore, overrode Roger's claim to the title and created William and Mary Baron and Baroness Stafford in 1640 and subsequently made them Viscount and Viscountess Stafford the following year. (Roger died in 1640 before he could contest his disinheritance.)

Thus the Stafford title came into a line of the Howard family of the Dukes of Norfolk. Though Mary Stafford Howard eventually inherited Stafford Castle and remaining lands on the death of her mother, the castle had been reduced to ruin by the Parliamentarians in the Civil War. William's mother, Aletheia Countess of Arundel, however, was a great heiress in her own right. (She was the daughter and eventually sole heiress of Gilbert 7th Earl of Shrewsbury.) After a quarrel with her eldest son she bequeathed to William and Mary much of the valuable Arundel Collection of art which she and her husband had formed in the reign of Charles I, her London house, Tart Hall near St James's Park, and estates round Shifnal in Shropshire.

Tart Hall remained the Stafford's London house down to the 1740s, while the Shifnal estate has descended with the title, like Stafford Castle, down to the present day.

Despite his peerage and his splendid inheritance William, Viscount Stafford had an unhappy life and tragic death on account of his strong Catholicism. Significant periods were spent in exile on the Continent or involved in lawsuits with his relations. Eventually, he was implicated in the Titus Oates Plot, falsely accused of treason and unjustly executed in 1680, the last of the Staffords, and the Howards, to meet this fate. His widow Mary was created a Countess for life by James II as a sort of apology and their son was made Earl of Stafford. There were four Catholic Earls of Stafford in the early 18th century but they lived partly on the Continent and frequently married into the French aristocracy, becoming more European nobility than English. They neglected and sold their English properties and demolished Tart Hall. On the death of the 4th Earl of Stafford in 1762, the earldom became extinct. The claim to the attainted barony of Stafford, Stafford Castle and the Shifnal estates, however, descended through the female line to the Jerninghams, an old-established Catholic family seated at Costessey Hall in Norfolk. Like the Stafford-Howards, the Jerninghams and their relations had strong Continental connections. In the second half of the 18th century, however, they emerged as one of the most interesting English Catholic families living in Norfolk and London, intelligent, social, and well-connected, working as improving landowners and active campaigners for Catholic Emancipation, their younger sons dabbling in literature and the Law. They were enriched by marriages to heiresses and the pioneering industrialisation of the Shifnal estates through the 18th-century development of the Shropshire coal and iron industries in the Ironbridge and Coalbrookdale area. They used this wealth to rebuild the ruins of Stafford Castle as a Picturesque folly and to reconstruct Costessey as an ambitious and pioneering house of the 19th-century gothic revival.

In the early 19th century, after a long campaign, the Jerninghams were able to reverse the attainder against Viscount Stafford by Act of Parliament and in 1825 they succeeded to the Barony of Stafford when George Jerningham became 8th Baron Stafford. His second son, Edward, married Marianne Smythe, the adopted daughter of Mrs Fitzherbert, the illegal wife of George IV. Mrs Fitzherbert reintroduced a royal connection into the family story, and foreshadowed the inheritance in the early 20th century of the Stafford barony by the Fitzherberts of Swynnerton Hall in Staffordshire when the Jerninghams, too, failed in the male line, and the title descended once again through a female heiress, together with Stafford Castle and the Shifnal estate and some of the Howard and Jerningham portraits and heirlooms. Thus in the 20th century, the barony of Stafford and Stafford Castle came to be vested once again in a native Staffordshire family and history seems to have come almost a full circle.

Emily Charlotte Stafford Jerningham, only surviving sister of the 10th and 11th (Stafford Jerningham) Barons Stafford married Basil Fitzherbert. Their son Major Francis Edward Fitzherbert DSO succeeded to the title, on the death of the 11th Baron, as 12th Lord Stafford. The present holder of the title is his grandson. The 19th-century interconnections between the Jerninghams and Fitzherberts are complicated by intermarriage. Basil Fitzherbert as well as being the husband of Emily Charlotte Jerningham (his first wife) also married (secondly, after Emily's death in 1881), her aunt-in-law, Emma Eliza, widow of the 9th Lord Stafford, and this was additional to the 'Marianne Smythe' connection. Marianne had married Edward Stafford Jerningham (second son of the 8th Lord Stafford) and so was mother of Emily Fitzherbert (wife of Basil) and grandmother of the 12th Lord Stafford.

I

The Origins of the Stafford Family
& Stafford Castle
1066-1300

⊱·⊰

MANY FAMILIES CLAIM, not always accurately, descent from an ancestor who came over to England after the Norman Conquest. The Staffords' claim to Norman ancestry, however, was true; in the 11th century they were granted property by William the Conqueror in Staffordshire and other counties. This was to become the nucleus of the greatest territorial estate in England in the course of the Middle Ages. The first English ancestor of the family was a Norman knight called Robert of Toeni (or Tonei, or Tosney) the youngest son of Roger de Toeni, a member of a Norman family which was closely connected with William the Conqueror. The de Toenis were the ducal standard-bearers in Normandy. Robert de Toeni was part of a second influx of Norman landowners into England. Immediately after the Battle of Hastings William had rewarded his victorious colleagues with grants of the lands of the defeated. A few years later, faced with outbreaks of revolt against Norman rule in England, there was more widespread replacement of English landowners with Normans.

After an insurrection at Stafford in 1070, which the Conqueror put down with characteristic firmness, ravaging much of the county, the confiscated lands there of Earl Edwin were granted to Robert, including a manor then known as Bradley (later known as Castle Church) and the hill overlooking the river four miles south-west of the burgh of Stafford. This site was of some strategic significance as it controlled the river-crossing on an important route from Wales to the Midlands of England and was a second line of defence against Welsh insurrection. It was no doubt a condition of the grant that Robert should build a stronghold on the hill there on the eastern fringe of his Bradley manor estate, within sight of the town.

The establishment of castles at key strategic points formed a significant part of William's plans for holding England after the Norman Conquest. They included a defensive chain along the south coast from Dover to Carisbrooke on the Isle of Wight including Bramber, Lewes and Arundel; and a ring round London of which the royal castle overlooking the Thames at Windsor was the chief. Elsewhere key points were identified and William's more trusted followers were granted lands in return for erecting castles on them. William himself built a series of royal castles in towns, to overawe the English, and he built his own royal castle within the burgh of Stafford two years after the 1070 revolt against Norman rule.

The history of the English branch of the Toeni family and the early history of their Stafford castle are both obscure. Robert, it is presumed, built the first castle at Bradley c.1086 but there is no documentary evidence and the story is confused by the existence of the two Stafford castles: a royal castle in the town as well as Robert's on the hill outside.[1] Domesday Book is inconclusive. While it does not record a castle on the hill at Bradley in 1086, there may have been a settlement there called Montevile or Montville. At the time of Domesday Book the royal castle in the town of Stafford is described as 'destructum', though it seems to have been still garrisoned. Robert's castle rose as the royal castle declined. In the reign of King Henry I there is documentary evidence that Stafford Castle was entrusted to William Pantulf, but this was probably the royal castle.

Robert Toeni's post-Conquest fortifications were of earth and timber and the Norman motte still survives though altered later in the Middle Ages.[2] By the time of Domesday Book in 1086 Robert was already calling himself 'Robert of Stafford'.

The first castle was of Norman motte and bailey plan, and contained a chapel as well as living quarters. The remains indicate that the original castle was built about a decade after the Norman Conquest and recent archaeological research convincingly suggests that Robert de Stafford's castle on the hill can be dated to c.1086-7.

Robert was the largest landowner in Staffordshire, and his castle was therefore a substantial affair. He artificially remodelled the hill to create a strong earth and timber castle with a motte and two baileys on a large scale. The fortifications and outworks covered an area of about fifteen acres. The motte was surrounded on the north and east by an inner bailey, with an outer bailey to the south-east. These were defended by complex and impressive earthworks with dry ditches and a counterscarp bank, of which traces remain. The village settlement (noted in Domesday Book) lay to the south-east, where the lines of three parallel roads are still visible, and St Mary's church is situated down below. Stafford Great Park lay to the north and east of the castle. This castle remained the principal residence of the family for the next hundred years.[3]

Robert de Stafford was one of the greater tenants-in-chief of Norman England. At the time of the Domesday Survey he is recorded as holding 70 manors in Staffordshire, over 25 in Warwickshire, over 20 in Lincolnshire, 10 in Oxfordshire, one in Worcestershire and one in Northamptonshire.[4] The bulk of his lands in Staffordshire lay on either side of the county town and were scattered rather than comprising a compact bloc. He was not given the borough, or a continuous belt of land round it. William the Conqueror deliberately 'witheld from Robert everything which might savour of earldom'. He was, however, the greatest private landowner in the shire, and held most of the lands there of the Saxon Earl of Mercia. He, his son and grandson after him were all sheriff of Staffordshire. From the beginning, therefore, they had a leading position in the county, and this was expressed in their new surname 'of Stafford'.

Though Robert de Toeni or Robert de Stafford (as it is simplest to call him) was rewarded by William I with the grant of Bradley and other manors in Staffordshire and elsewhere, these, as has been seen, were deliberately not all concentrated in one area but scattered. This was a conscious policy on the part of William the Conqueror who did not want Robert to build up a strong regional power base which might pose a threat to the Crown. William did not completely trust him. His father had rebelled against the Duke in Normandy, and William did not want the son to be in a position to do the same in England. He, therefore, tempered his generosity to Robert by rewarding him well, but not with a concentrated fief.

Nevertheless, Robert and his immediate successors claimed to be titular Lords of Stafford. His descendants, however, were prevented from controlling the town by their comparatively slender finances and modest military following. As the King intended, they were forced to be loyal out of necessity. Over the succeeding three generations they proved themselves able and dependable. They continued to live at Stafford Castle, and at some date in the 12th century a small stone keep was built on top of the motte.

Few personal details of these early Staffords survive. References are restricted to occasional grants of land, witnesses of charters or burials. So only the most basic framework of their lives can now be known. Towards the end of his life Robert de Stafford became a monk and entered the Abbey at Evesham where he died in 1088 and was almost certainly buried. Throughout his life he had been a generous patron of monastic foundations. As well as Evesham he was a benefactor of Conches in Normandy and Wootton Wawen Priory in Warwickshire, and the founder of Stone Priory in Staffordshire.[5]

He was succeeded by his son Nicholas de Stafford who was a benefactor of Kenilworth Priory and who died c.1138. He was buried at Stone Priory, the monastic foundation which continued to have strongest connections with the Stafford family; it was founded by them and benefited from the family's patronage and protection throughout the Middle Ages. Many members of the family were buried there. Nicholas in turn was succeeded by his son and grandson, both called Robert. The former was still alive in the reign of Henry II, and was sheriff of Staffordshire from 1155 to 1160. The latter died c.1193 while on crusade in the Holy Land with Richard the Lionheart. With him the male line of the English Toeni Staffords came to an end, leaving a sole female heir.[6]

1 The Stafford arms. Gules a
chevron Or. (From Percy's Roll,
College of Arms)

Robert de Stafford III was succeeded by his sister Millicent who married Hervey
Bagot, a sub-tenant of the Staffords and almost certainly the grandson of Bagot who
held Bramshall, Staffordshire, from Robert de Stafford at the time of the Domesday
Survey. Millicent died shortly after 1225 and is also buried at Stone Priory. Their son,
like his father called Hervey, took the name Stafford and is the male ancestor of the
subsequent Stafford family. In the 13th century Stafford Castle declined in importance
and lost its former prestige, as did the Bagot Stafford family. The evidence suggests
that the Staffords failed to maintain their original influence and suffered from declining
finances, though they regularly provided military service for the King on the Welsh
marches. Recent archaeological investigations have shown that, unlike many other
English Norman castles, Stafford was not modernised at this time, nor improved in
the century after its original foundation by replacing original timber defences with
stone curtain walls, towers and a gatehouse. Instead, some of the castle's defensive
ditches were filled in.[7] There is no evidence that the site was abandoned, however, and
the dependent 'vill of the castle' continued to be occupied.

The 14th century saw the Stafford fortunes actively restored, and the progressive
and continuous aggrandisement of the family through three successive generations.
Slowly the Staffords achieved a place in national affairs, in which they were able to
display military and administrative skills. This brought them royal favour and titles and
in due course the opportunity to make very good marriages to heiresses. In the late
13th century they became Barons Stafford, in the 14th century Earls of Stafford and
in the 15th century Dukes of Buckingham.

Like many medieval families, the Staffords rose through warfare and marriage.
They were involved in the Welsh wars of Edward I, where they fought for the King.

2 Stafford Castle – reconstruction of the appearance of the Norman castle by P. Scollins. (By kind permission of the Friends of Stafford Castle)

3 Aerial view of Stafford Castle showing extent of Norman earthworks. (John Darlington © Stafford Borough Council)

Nicholas (the great-grandson of Millicent) served in Wales repeatedly from 1277 onwards and was killed there in 1287 under a falling wall at the siege of Deresloyn Castle; he, too, was buried at the family priory at Stone. He is consistently described as Baron de Stafford, though his son, Edmund, was the first to receive a writ of summons to Parliament, the defining feature of the baronage.

Edmund also made the first of the family's many notable marriages to heiresses. His wife was Margaret, daughter of Ralph Lord Basset. As a result of this marriage, the Staffords were eventually to inherit part of the Basset estates in Norfolk and the Midlands, worth £200 per annum. This was still in the future. Edmund's increased stature and his military service to the Crown were recognised and rewarded in 1299 when he was summoned to Parliament as 1st Lord Stafford. He, too, fought for Edward I in Wales and Scotland, and was present at the coronation of Edward II on 18 January 1307/8. Edmund established the Stafford family in the peerage of England and as prominent military commanders. This was a foundation which his son, Ralph, built on magnificently in the following century, when the outbreak of the Hundred Years War with France provided great opportunities for advancement through military service overseas with its potential for wages, profit, loot and ransoms.[8]

II

Earls and Bishops

❧ · ❧

THE HUNDRED YEARS WAR between England and France in the 14th century provided a useful means of enrichment for aspiring nobles and knights, and also the chance of royal notice and favour with the opportunity to make good marriages to heiresses. It was an opportunity which Ralph 1st Lord Stafford exploited to the full. Ralph, who was born on 28 September 1301, succeeded his father in about 1308 and received his lands after coming of age in December 1323.[1] Like his father before him he was active in military affairs from an early age. As a young man he played an extensive role in the wars in Scotland, leading military expeditions there, composed of troops raised in and around his Midlands estates. The reputation he achieved on the Scottish borders brought him favour at Court and, from the beginning, he was one of Edward III's most trusted military captains.

He married twice. His first wife Katherine was the daughter of Sir John Hastang of Chebsey, Staffordshire. After her death he married again. His second marriage to Margaret Audley c.1336 was a great coup. He was able to bring this off thanks to the support of the King and this in turn was earned with his military dash and achievement. Margaret, the daughter of Hugh Audley, was one of the heiresses to the estate of her grandfather, Gilbert de Clare, Earl of Gloucester and Hereford, one of the greatest magnates in early medieval England. On Gilbert's death childless in 1317 the de Clare lands had been divided between his three sisters. Margaret, the second sister, who was married to Hugh Audley, received the Lordship of Newport and other lands across England worth £2,314 p.a. Their only daughter, called Margaret after her mother, was the heiress to all this.

After the death of his first wife, Ralph Stafford saw his opportunity and daringly abducted Margaret Audley from her house at Thaxted, Essex in an armed raid, and married her. Her father, Hugh Audley, not surprisingly was enraged by this audacious act, but Edward III intervened to protect Ralph from his father-in-law's anger. The

4 Brass of Sir Hugh Hastings at Elsing church, Norfolk with a portrait of Ralph 1st Earl of Stafford on the right. (NMR)

King arranged a rapprochement between Hugh and Ralph. After his anger subsided, Hugh came to see that his new son-in-law was not unworthy; he was a popular, brave and able lord. Nine years after the marriage, in 1343, the two men were reconciled enough for Hugh to settle all his property, both the Audley and the de Clare lands, on Ralph, Margaret and their heirs. Hugh Audley died three years later and Ralph came into his huge inheritance in 1346. At the same time he inherited another fortune from his grandmother, Alice Corbet. This was the lordship of Caus on the border between Shropshire and Montgomery. With an income of £265 per annum, this additional property reinforced Ralph Stafford's position as one of the leading lords on the Welsh Marches. The combined inheritances made him one of the richest men in England with an estimated income from his English and Welsh estates of £3,350 per annum.[2]

His landed revenue was only a part of his total income for, in addition, Ralph benefited from generous grants from the Crown, and the profits of his military campaigns, especially the French Wars. It is impossible now to calculate how much he benefited from ransoms, booty, plunder and other rewards, but it must have been a substantial amount of money.

The outbreak of the Hundred Years War in 1338, when Edward III – with the support of Flanders and Burgundy – claimed the French throne by right of his mother, provided Ralph with an unequalled opportunity. He had already proved his mettle as a military leader in Scotland, where he had been created a Knight Banneret in 1327. Edward III held him in enough favour to have made him Steward of the King's Household and a member of the Privy Council. Ralph accompanied Edward on his first campaign to Flanders from 1338 to 1348. As well as his military command there he also fulfilled various diplomatic roles, including embassies to the Counts of Hainault and Gueldres to encourage their support for the English side in the opening moves of the campaign.

Ralph was noted for his valour and daring, and was to acquit himself with considerable distinction in France. Success on the battlefield, and the consequent favour and trust of the King, enabled him to execute the Audley marriage. By these means he established the Staffords as one of the leading families of medieval England, both very rich and very well-connected. He raised them from a Midlands family of local importance to a great power in the Kingdom: soldiers, diplomats and statesmen who helped mould the history of their times. Ralph's achievement was consolidated by his successors who matched his acts by daring military leadership and successful marriages to heiresses over successive generations throughout the next two centuries – though not without tragic consequences for themselves.

Ralph Stafford took part in the first major English victory of the Hundred Years War: in 1339 at Cadsant in Flanders. He was a member of the King's Army at Vironfosse throughout 1339, as is recorded in Froissart's chronicle of the Wars. He returned to England with the King in November 1340, but two years later led reinforcements to Brittany and defeated Charles de Blois on 30 September 1341. He was captured by the enemy at the siege of Vannes in Brittany but was successfully exchanged for a French prisoner, Olivier de Clisson (or Clichon), under the terms of the Truce of Malestroit between the English and the French. On 20 May 1344 he took part in the embassy to Pope Clement VI at Avignon in connection with the short-lived peace, one of several diplomatic missions on which he was engaged at this time.

On 25 February 1345 he was appointed Seneschal of Aquitaine and joined the Earl of Derby's campaign in Gascony, commanding the successful water-borne attack which captured Bergerac on the Dordogne. Following the surrender of Aiguillon he was appointed governor of the town responsible for its refortification. He patched the broken walls with wine casks filled with stones and successfully defended the place against the French King's son, John, Duke of Normandy (himself later King of France). He played a prominent part at the battle of Crecy in 1346 which saw the decisive defeat of the French. He then returned to England, while the English army settled in for the long winter siege of Calais; while there he was sent by the King on a mission to Scotland in 1347. He was back in France, however, for the surrender of Calais and with the Earl of Warwick was responsible for the ceremonial reception of the keys of the town and castle. In 1348 he was created one of the founder Knights of the Garter by Edward III in the chivalric ceremony at Windsor Castle which celebrated the successful high point of the King's military conquests in France, with the English in possession of the whole of the western part of the country from Calais to Gascony.[3]

During his leave in England in 1347, Ralph embarked on a project at Stafford Castle to erect an up-to-date tower house on the old motte which was part flattened to accommodate a larger building. He made an agreement in 1347/8 with John de Barcestre, mason, for building the new castle in local stone. A medieval copy of the contract survives in the Stafford Record Office.

> This indenture made between Sir Ralph, Baron of Stafford, of the one part, and Master John of Burcestre, mason, of the other part, witnesses that it is agreed between them that the said Master John shall build a castle on the mound within the manor of Stafford, in length, breadth, and height, with towers, rooms, bedchambers, chapel, privies, chimneys, loopholes, windows, doors, and gates, together with vaulting, according to the plan and orders of the said Sir Ralph, and that all the towers shall be higher than the hall and the bedrooms by ten feet, and that the commencement of the wall shall be seven statute feet, without gaps or insubstantial work. Five marks shall be allowed for each perch, and each perch shall be 24 statute feet. And the loopholes, vaults, chimneys, and doors shall be measured in all places within the walls. And the said Sir Ralph shall cause stone, sand, and lime to be carried as far as the foot of the mound. And the said Sir Ralph shall provide scaffolding, ladders, hurdles, beams, buckets, timbers, planks, and vessels needed for the work, fuel for his [i.e. Master John's] household, himself and his people, and hay for his horses. And the said Master John shall cause the stone, and all other necessary things that pertain to the work to be carried from the foot of the mound to the top, and continue until the work on the said castle shall be quite complete. In witness to which agreement the two parties have interchangeably set their seals to these indentures. And because Sir Ralph's seal is not available, the seals of master William of

Colton and of John of Pickstock are affixed. Written at Stafford Castle on Saint Hilary's day, the twenty first year of the reign of King Edward, the third after the Conquest [i.e., 13 January 1347/8].[4]

He also obtained a licence to crenellate in 1348, by this date something of a formality. Builders' wages for the castle continued to be paid annually until 1368, when the new work was completed. Ralph's new castle was a compact, rectangular building with four octagonal corner towers, a fifth tower in the centre of the north side and a central great hall, all laid out on symmetrical lines. It is thought that the new castle incorporated at one end the walls of the old stone keep. The lower parts of the walls still survive and give an idea of Ralph's new castle-house. It was as much a symbol of chivalry and lordship as a serious fortification. Ralph was no doubt inspired in its design by the castles he had seen in France. Its sophisticated symmetrical appearance showed an awareness of the decorative and symbolic qualities of the castle-style just like Edward III's own great rebuilding of Windsor Castle, or the works of other military commanders in the French wars, such as Bodiam in Sussex. At this date a licence to crenellate was as much a symbol of lordship as a military necessity. The new Stafford Castle was a demonstration of Ralph's enhanced status at the *caput*, or seat, of his barony after his successful campaigns in France and the great Audley-de Clare inheritance. From his battlements at Stafford, Ralph could see the country for twenty or thirty miles around, including his new lands at the Lordship of Caus on the Welsh border, to the west.

A further mark of Ralph's enhanced status and his new wealth was his creation by Edward III on 5 March 1350/1 as Earl of Stafford. The Audley-de Clare inheritance provided him with an income capable of supporting the greater dignity of an earldom. As an extra mark of royal favour, the King granted him, in addition to the earldom, a pension for life of 1,000 marks a year. As a very wealthy and powerful man, Ralph was able to arrange good marriages for all his children, and to consolidate the Stafford family's rise a rung up the ladder of the peerage.

The eldest son was betrothed to Matilda, daughter of Henry Earl of Derby and Duke of Lancaster, Ralph's commander in Aquitaine and one of the most celebrated military leaders of the day. This alliance did not bear fruit, however, as the boy died young. Ralph's second son (and eventual heir) Hugh married the daughter of Thomas Beauchamp, Earl of Warwick, another prominent commander in the Hundred Years War. In this way, the French campaigns gave Ralph the opportunity to make and cement distinguished martial alliances between his own family and other leading members of the English peerage. He was the first of his line to achieve national recognition in England and France as soldier, diplomat and statesman.[5]

Not that he rested on his laurels after having achieved an earldom, for the following year, 1352, he was back in France where he served as Lieutenant and Captain of Aquitaine, and took part in further military campaigns in the north of the country. In 1355 he went again to Scotland, but was soon the same year back in France

5 Tonbridge Castle, Kent – the Gatehouse, built *c.*1300; the *caput* of the Kent estates which formed part of the Audley inheritance. (NMR)

as part of Edward III's new campaign there, where Stafford's brother, Sir Richard Stafford, was also campaigning and had become Seneschal of Gascony. Ralph, Earl of Stafford, was one of the English commissioners who drew up the Treaty of Bretigny, which marked the end of the first phase of the Hundred Years War, on 11 May 1360.[6]

In 1361 Ralph accompanied Lionel, the future Duke of Clarence, on a campaign to Ireland and in 1367 he contracted to supply the King with a hundred men at arms for a yearly stipend of 1,000 marks provided out of the customs revenue. His mobility is striking, with annual summer campaigns in France, winters in England managing his estates or waiting on the King, interspersed with embassies in France, or campaigns to Scotland and Ireland. In the end, worn out with constant military service, he died at Tonbridge Castle in Kent, part of his Audley inheritance, on 31 August 1372 aged 73, a good age by medieval standards. He was buried at Tonbridge.

In his lifetime he showed all the signs of conventional medieval piety, continuing as a benefactor of Stone Priory and himself founding the Austin Friars in Stafford in 1344. The Austin Friars, both in Stafford and London, continued to be a favoured religious order of the Stafford family down to the early 16th century. Ralph was also a patron of St John's Hospital in Stafford.[7]

The medieval Staffords, in addition to their military prowess, also produced a number of distinguished churchmen including two English bishops. Edmund, the second son of Sir Richard Stafford (the Seneschal of Gascony, i.e. the nephew of the 1st Earl) entered Holy Orders. He was born in 1344, and soon after ordination he

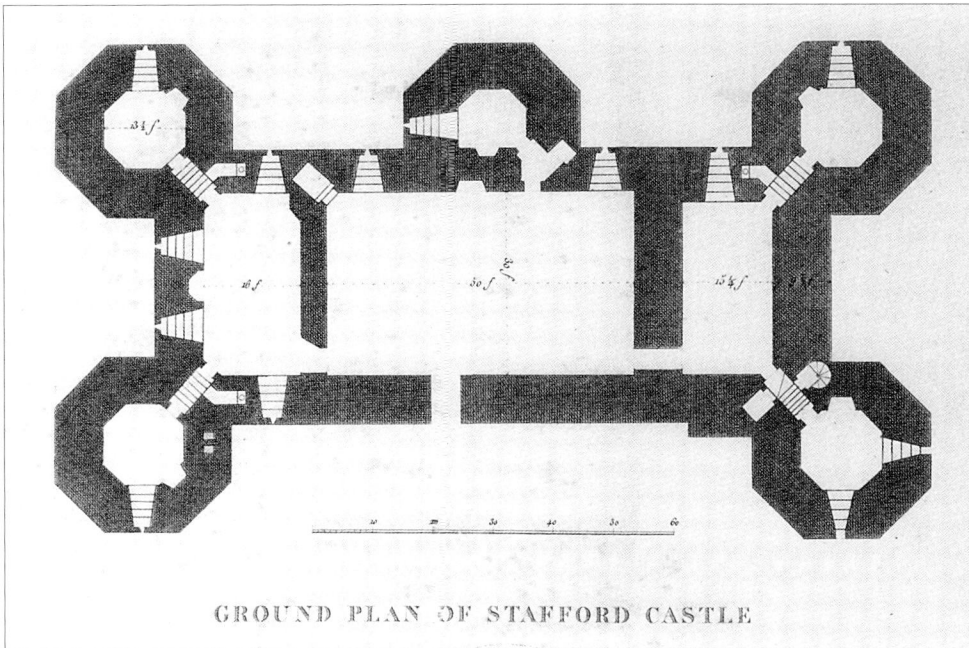

GROUND PLAN OF STAFFORD CASTLE

6 Stafford Castle. Plan of the keep rebuilt by the 1st Earl of Stafford in 1348 as a French-influenced fortified house. (Salt Library, Stafford)

obtained a prebend of Lichfield Cathedral through the influence of his family. As a well-educated man, like most leading medieval ecclesiastics, he combined his clerical duties with government administration. In about 1389, he was appointed Keeper of the Privy Seal and on 15 January 1394/5 he became Bishop of Exeter.

At first he was too busy in London with affairs of state to visit his diocese. On 23 October 1396 he was appointed Lord Chancellor, a post he held till the abdication of Richard II in 1399 when Henry Bolingbroke took the throne. He was also removed from the Privy Council at that time by the new King Henry IV; this gave him the opportunity to reside in his diocese. Early in 1400 he was able to settle at Exeter and to undertake his episcopal duties in earnest. This he did with the thoroughness that had marked him as a public servant. He spent a whole year on an intensive visitation of his episcopal territory in Devon and Cornwall, confirming his flock, dealing with abuses and generally putting everything into order. In January 1401 he was recalled to London where he was restored as Lord Chancellor, a post he held for a year during which one of his clergy, Robert Rugge, acted as his vicar-general at Exeter.

In 1403 he returned to Exeter again, where he spent the last 16 years of his life. He was noted as a learned man and a great patron of scholarship. He was also a generous benefactor of Exeter College, Oxford, which had been founded as a hall by

7 Tomb of Bishop Edmund Stafford, Lord Chancellor of England, at Exeter Cathedral, 1419. (Courtauld)

his predecessor, and which he enlarged, paying for new buildings and giving books to the library. He died on 3 September 1419 aged 75 and is buried at Exeter Cathedral.[8]

The other Stafford bishop rose even higher in the episcopal hierarchy and became Archbishop of Canterbury from 1443 to 1452. This was John Stafford, a cousin of the main line of the family. His parentage is somewhat mysterious, but he seems to have been the natural son of Sir Humphrey Stafford of Southwick, Wiltshire, by Emma of North Bradley and was born about 1385.[9] He was educated at Oxford, and he too was busy in politics as Keeper of the Privy Seal and Lord Chancellor. He was the first holder of the latter office to be styled 'Lord Chancellor', perhaps a sign of the concern for dignities which his contemporaries noted. He was considered a clever and generous man, noted for his hospitality. He was a cautious rather than a brilliant administrator. The Victorian historian, William Stubbs, summed up his achievement: '… if he had done little good, he had done no harm'.[10] He, like many of his family, was a keen builder and reconstructed part of the palace at Croydon, Surrey, where the mid-15th-century Great Hall survives from his time. It has a noble timber roof with big arched braces, collar beams and wind braces, all splendidly moulded. The Stafford knot badge can still be seen carved on the stone corbels.

Ralph, 1st Earl of Stafford was succeeded by his younger son, Hugh, who was born in about 1342. He followed in his father's footsteps in France and served in Aquitaine in the retinue of the Black Prince during 1363-66 and also took part in the expedition

8 The Great Hall at Croydon Palace rebuilt by Archbishop John Stafford.

9 The splendid timber roof of the Hall at Croydon. (NMR)

to Spain. He was summoned to Parliament in his father's lifetime as Baron Stafford. In 1373 he took part in John of Gaunt's army of invasion into France and two years later joined the Duke of Brittany's forces in Brittany. He was created a Knight of the Garter in 1375, three years after his accession to the earldom. The 2nd Earl of Stafford belonged to the Court party and was a member of the enlarged council which advised the young Richard II. He officiated as carver at the Coronation Banquet, a ceremonial honour. He was also involved in the practical side of government. As well as being a member of the Privy Council he was employed as a member of various Lords' commissions to do with matters such as the public finances and the regulation of the Royal Household. Hugh Stafford was a popular figure who played an active part in national affairs. This did not, however, protect him from personal tragedy.

In 1385 he took part in the expedition to Scotland, accompanied by his eldest son Ralph. The latter was killed in Yorkshire by the King's half-brother John Holland, Earl of Huntingdon, later Duke of Exeter. He murdered Ralph in revenge for the death of his favourite esquire, who was killed in a brawl by one of Stafford's archers. Richard II promised Hugh that he would not pardon the murderer, but eventually did.[11] Embittered by this, Hugh decided to leave England. He resigned his public commissions and departed on a pilgrimage to Jerusalem, a hazardous journey in the later Middle Ages. He spent twelve months on the outward journey and succeeded in visiting the Holy Places, but died at Rhodes in 1386 on his return voyage. His body was brought home and buried at Stone Priory. Before leaving, he had settled his estates in a series of extensive enfeoffments, or legal trusts, intended to protect them during the minority of his heir.

The 2nd Earl was to be succeeded in turn by his second, third and fourth sons: Thomas, William and Edmund. Thomas 3rd Earl of Stafford came of age in 1390 and was knighted on 23 April of that year. In the most spectacular marital connection in the history of the Stafford family he married Lady Anne Plantagenet, daughter of Thomas of Woodstock, Duke of Gloucester, grandson of King Edward III. They had no children, however, and Thomas Stafford died in 1392, being buried at Stone, next to his father.[12] The earldom then passed to the next boy, William, but he was still a minor and died three years later aged only seventeen. So he in turn was succeeded by the third brother Edmund as 5th Earl of Stafford. He too was still a minor, but the Duke of Gloucester had kept the wardship of the two younger Staffords after the death of his son-in-law, Thomas, their elder brother. Gloucester now remarried his daughter Lady Anne, with a special royal licence, to Edmund Stafford. (She was, of course, Edmund's widowed sister-in-law). Thus was finally achieved the splendid but ultimately fatal alliance which raised the Staffords to the highest ranks of the English nobility and made them connections of the royal family itself. It was to bring them both glory and death.

At stake was a huge inheritance, larger than anything the Staffords had so far acquired by inheritance, warfare and marriage. Lady Anne was an heiress twice over.

10 The arms of Archbishop Stafford (beneath the angel corbel). The engrailed border marks his illegitimate descent, and the mitre his episcopal rank. (NMR)

From her brother she was heiress to the earldom of Buckingham (created for her father) and property worth £1,000 p.a. From her mother Eleanor de Bohun (who had died in 1399) she was also sole heiress to half the de Bohun estates. The other half had been inherited by Henry Duke of Lancaster, now King Henry IV.[13]

Humphrey de Bohun, Earl of Hereford, Earl of Essex and Earl of Northampton had died without issue in 1361. His lands had then passed to his nephew who in turn had no sons but two daughters. Eleanor, the elder, married Thomas, Duke of Gloucester, and Mary, the younger, Henry IV. After long drawn out negotiations, in which the estates were divided and re-divided, half went to the King and half to Anne Countess of Stafford. As a result Edmund 5th Earl of Stafford was exceedingly rich, the holder of vast estates across England, between Holderness in the East Riding of Yorkshire and Newport in South Wales, between Tonbridge in Kent and Caus on the Shropshire border. This great patrimony had come to the Staffords over three generations from other noble families less successful in avoiding dynastic failure, the accidents of war or political attainder.

Even at the beginning, however, the great new inheritance brought problems. No sooner had Edmund and his advisors started to re-organise and consolidate his estates, merging the new with his existing holdings, than the Crown started to query the original partition. This led to protracted law suits in favour of Henry V which led to the inheritance being repartitioned and re-settled in 1421. The terms of this settlement served to remind future generations of Staffords of friction with the Crown to which they had previously been loyal and from whose bounty and protection they had hitherto benefited so greatly.

At first sight the new division seemed to offer even greater opportunities for consolidation and expansion. The Bohun castles and Lordships of Hay, Huntingdon and Brecon in Wales seemed to marry well with the Staffords' existing Marcher lordships and to enhance their authority in Wales. The problem, however, which soon became apparent, was that general disorder and popular resistance made it impossible to collect the full revenues from the Welsh estates. Future generations of Staffords were to be out of pocket as a result and were forced to resort to high-handed management policies which gave them a reputation for arrogant disregard for the King's law.[14]

Though there were problems with the estates which were to take many years to sort out, and the dowager Duchess of Gloucester was to hold much of the property in dower till her death in 1339, the Buckingham-Bohun inheritance nevertheless transformed the stature of the Stafford family. Edmund's own paternal estates had been well-managed during his minority and the eighteen years of wardship by the councillors who had been appointed by his father's foresight for the purpose. It was these councillors who finally secured for the Staffords their share of the Basset inheritance after long lawsuits and nearly a century after the original Basset-Stafford marriage had made them heirs to that property. It did Edmund little good, however. He was only Earl of Stafford for eight years from 1395, for he was killed fighting for Henry IV against Harry Hotspur (Percy) at the Battle of Shrewsbury in 1403. Four successive heads of the family and one heir from the 5th Earl onwards were to meet similarly violent ends, dying either on the scaffold or the battlefield during the course of the 15th and the opening years of the 16th centuries.

III

The Dukes of Buckingham

❦ · ❦

H UMPHREY STAFFORD (1402-1460), named after his Bohun great-uncle, was only one year old when in 1403 he inherited the earldom of Stafford from his father. He was also the heir to the earldom of Buckingham as part of his mother's inheritance from the Duke of Gloucester (her brother having died without male heirs). This title dated back to 1377 when her father was created Earl of Buckingham.

There were lawsuits about the Buckingham earldom as well as the division of the estates but Anne Countess of Buckingham and Stafford had good lawyers who successfully defended her claim to the earldom, as well as her share of the property. On her death in 1438 Humphrey inherited an income of £4,500 (gross) p.a., in addition to that of £1,500 p.a. from his father.[1] Humphrey thus became one of the richest and most powerful landowners in England. This together with his royal descent as great-grandson and heir-general of Edward III, as well as a lifetime's service to the Crown, made possible his creation as 1st Duke of Buckingham six years later. Dukedoms, in England, which had been instituted by Edward I as titles for his children, continued throughout the Middle Ages to reflect, in the main, royal relationships as well as pre-eminent landed wealth. Humphrey himself married Lady Anne Nevill, daughter of Ralph 1st Earl of Westmorland, sister of the Earl of Salisbury and aunt of Edward IV.

There are few characters in the Middle Ages for whom enough material survives to write a personal biography in the modern sense. It is only possible to approach them obliquely, through their estate accounts and finances (the careful and prudent management of which was the basis of their status and public standing) and the bare outline of their official and military careers as recorded in the State Papers and contemporary chronicles. This is just as true of Humphrey, 1st Duke of Buckingham, as of his noble predecessors and his 15th-century successors.

He continued to play the prominent role in state and military affairs established by the 1st Earl of Stafford. He was employed in a series of diplomatic missions to

11 Butler Bowden chasuble made for the marriage of Edmund, 5th Earl of Stafford to
Lady Anne Plantagenet in 1398. It is embellished with the Stafford knot and other heraldry.
(Victoria & Albert Museum)

the King of France, and was involved in all the attempts to reach a settlement there between 1435 and 1447; he also occupied a number of important offices in England. He was a member of the lay judicial body which investigated the claims of sorcery against Alianore, Duchess of Gloucester. As High Steward, he presided over the trial of the Earl of Devonshire in March 1454. He was Captain of Calais, Constable of Dover Castle and Warden of the Cinque Ports. He was one of the Commission of Peers appointed in 1454 to create the King's infant son Prince of Wales and three years later was made responsible for supervising the prince's education. Between January 1423 and his death on 10 July 1460 he was appointed to 45 Commissions of the Peace in 16 separate counties, 24 Commissions of Oyer and Terminer and 47 special commissions. He occupied an important intermediate position, by reason of his family connections, between the Lancastrian and Yorkist parties, and in the mid-15th century he and his relations controlled the government for a period.

He earned a reputation as a moderate and conscientious man, loyal to the person of the monarch and opposed to violence, but lacking in strength of character, leadership and decisiveness and over-concerned with procedures and ceremonial. His presence on an official body often lent dignity to murky proceedings. His impartiality or aloofness had a fatalistic quality about it. In the early 1450s when his influence was at its zenith, when he and his half-brothers, the Bourchiers, controlled the government, he proved ineffective and failed to achieve a compromise between the Queen's party and the Duke of York, as the constitutional and political crisis developed. Though angered by the sack of Ludlow by royal troops he made no attempt to stop the pillage. He relinquished Sandwich and Kent, where his territorial influence was paramount, without any effort. Finally, he seems to have died with no attempt to defend himself; he was killed standing outside his tent at Northampton in 1460.[2]

As a young man he played a part in Henry V's great military adventure in France. On the renewal of the Hundred Years War he served in various capacities, just as his grandfather had done under King Edward III. He was present at the sieges of Melun and Meaux in 1420. 'This Humphrey was retained to serve the King in his Wars beyond the sea in [the 9th year of Henry V] by Indenture.'[3] In 1428 he had in his pay in France 97 men at arms and 240 archers. He maintained an interest in military affairs in France until about 1442, though thereafter the increasingly dangerous political situation at home occupied his attentions.[4]

He was knighted by Henry V on 22 April 1421. The following year he was granted 'livery' of his lands marking the formal end of his minority. Throughout his life he was to be loyal to the Lancastrian dynasty, even though after the early death of Henry V its representative, Henry VI, was first a minor, then a pious mediocrity, and intermittently mad. Humphrey was appointed to the King's Council in February 1424 when aged only 22, and he became a prominent figure at Court, being partly responsible in 1426 for reconciling the two senior figures in the Regency, Cardinal Beaufort, who supported peace in France, and Duke Humphrey of Gloucester, who wanted to

12 Lady Catherine Stafford, Countess of Westmorland, from the 15th-century Corby Castle altar frontal. (Victoria & Albert Museum)

continue the war. He was appointed a Knight of the Garter in 1429 on the occasion of Henry VI's marriage to Margaret of Anjou. He was the third of his race to receive that honour. In 1430 he accompanied Henry VI to France for his French coronation and was made Constable of France and Governor of Paris in August of that year.[5] On the renewed outbreak of fighting, he commanded the campaigns in Brie where he captured various strongholds. When subsequently relieved of these commands by the King's uncle, the Duke of Bedford, he was made Lieutenant General of Normandy. In 1431 he was created Count of Perche by Henry VI and Captain of Bellesme Castle, a Norman stronghold, to add to his English titles.[6] The following year he returned to England, but in August 1436 was back on the Continent for the short and fruitless summer campaign in Flanders.

Between 1435 and 1447 he was connected with all attempts to reach a peace settlement with France at the end of the Hundred Years War. In 1435, as a member of the Privy Council, he was part of the delegation led by his brother-in-law, John Earl of Huntingdon, and subscribed his name to the final agreement. This amounted to an apprenticeship in Anglo-French diplomacy. In 1439 he was a member of Cardinal Beaufort's embassy to France alongside his half-brother, Bishop Bourchier and three other ecclesiastics. They met the French on 28 June at Newnham Bridge. Negotiations broke down, however, over the English refusal to consider any waiver to Henry VI's title as King of France. (It remained one of the dignities of the King of England down to the Treaty of Paris in 1800.) Beaufort's embassy was the last time that England had a strong negotiating hand, even though the embassy ended in deadlock. Stafford was impressed by Cardinal Beaufort's astuteness and magnificence, and it has been suggested that he modelled some of his own public persona on the Cardinal's. He certainly shared with Beaufort a concern for dignities and ceremonial, though such an interest was typical of his class and period.

At the next round of negotiations six years later when in July 1445 a French Embassy came to London, the Duke of Suffolk was in charge of treating with its delegates and Maine was ceded to France in shameful circumstances. Stafford was distrustful of Suffolk and took little part in the actual negotiation, restricting himself to ceremonial duties and acting as host to the French delegates on behalf of the King. He even conducted the French on a tour of the royal tombs in Westminster Abbey.[7] By this date nearly all the English conquests in France had vanished except for Calais itself and its immediate hinterland.

Stafford himself was appointed Captain or Constable of the town of Calais, the Tower of Rysbank and Lieutenant of the Calais Marches in 1442. The soldiers in the Calais garrison were on the verge of mutiny and he had to pay them himself out of his own pocket, pending reimbursement by the Treasury. He held the post for ten years. This was an important office and gave the holder considerable strategic leverage on English affairs. It offered control of a considerable military garrison, as well as jurisdiction over an important economic centre. Calais was for England the gateway to the Continent, especially France and Burgundy, and was the entrepôt of much of England's wool trade. It was therefore of strategical and political importance in a period of political instability and upheaval. On the other hand the responsibility for military security at the time of English defeat in France posed a great burden, and this was exacerbated by the semi-mutinous state of the badly paid garrison. The efficient exercise of the duties of Captain meant exile from the Court and public affairs in England.

Successful Captains of Calais required strong characters, outstanding military ability and large financial resources of their own to pay the garrison on a regular basis to bridge the gaps between intermittent grants of Crown monies from England. Stafford had the position, the military experience and the financial backing for the job. He managed efficiently, but lacked the vision to use his role there to decisive advantage in English affairs, unlike his successor, the more ruthless Earl of Warwick, who master-minded the Yorkist invasion of Kent in 1459, and the Yorkist coup, from Calais.

Stafford did not leave England to take over at Calais for nearly a year after his appointment, but he employed an able soldier, Sir Thomas Kyriel, to oversee the fortifications and garrison for him. A crisis in August 1442 with symptoms of mutiny over arrears of pay – the soldiers seized the wools to enforce acknowledgement of their demands – precipitated Stafford to take personal charge. He travelled to Calais in October, having obtained licences to take with him money, plate and jewels to the

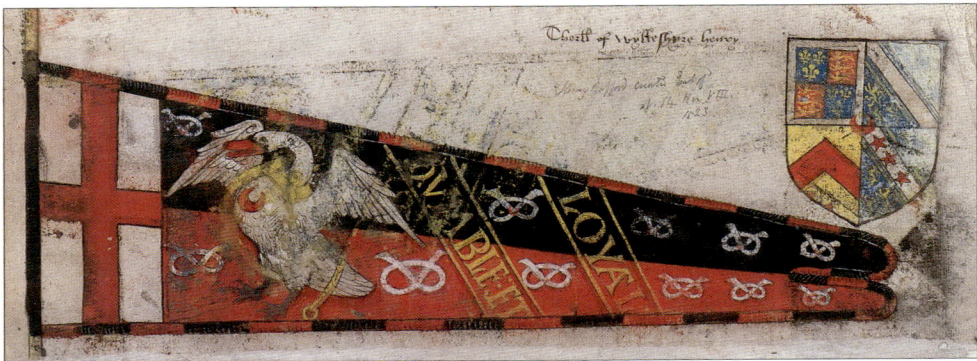

13 Stafford knot badge worn on their livery by Stafford retainers. (College of Arms)

value of 5,000 marks. On 12 October 1442 he obtained a grant of jewels pledged by the King worth 1,000 marks to be paid the following Easter which was a clever post-dated cheque on Stafford's part.[8]

His appearance in person with supplies of money alleviated the situation and having resolved things there he returned to England, but was back in Calais again in March 1443. By June that year, the wages of the garrison were again causing problems, and he secured an order from the Council for £3,401 out of the customs. For two years he had devoted the greater part of his time to personal supervision of Calais. From 1444, however, with his elevation to the dukedom of Buckingham, his priorities changed and he ceased to be so hands-on, delegating his duties at Calais to a lieutenant. By 1449 the payment of the garrison had once again fallen into arrears and the farm of the customs in Calais was granted to him in part payment of the money which he had personally supplied to the garrison. He surrendered the captaincy on 2 April 1451, a little ahead of the original proposed termination of his office. He obviously found the captaincy a tie when political circumstances necessitated his presence in England. The financial drain of subsidising the garrison was also an embarrassment. In 1451 he was owed £19, 395 'or thereabout' in arrears of salary and payment of the garrison.[9]

Attempts to receive payment of this debt occupied him for the rest of his life, and there is no evidence that full settlement was ever made by the Crown. Parliament granted him in lieu of payment 'all customs and subsidies coming or going on all goods in Sandwich and places belonging thereto'. He was also to receive six shillings and eight pence levied on every sack of wool in every part of the kingdom until the arrears had been paid. He appointed his own Collector of Customs, Richard Cook, at Sandwich, Kent. This large stake in the revenue of the port there complemented and reinforced his large landed interest in Kent. This was further strengthened by his purchase of the office of Constable of Dover Castle and Warden of the Cinque Ports from James Fiennes, Lord Saye and Sele, on 4 July 1450. The purchase was ratified by Letters Patent on 12 June 1452.[10]

14 Dover Castle. The 1st Duke of Buckingham became the Constable of Dover Castle and Warden of the Cinque Ports in 1452.

Strategically and politically this was an astute bargain. Apart from an annual salary of £300, it gave him control of the Channel between Kent and Calais and therefore of the main communications with France and Flanders, without the disadvantage of being out of England itself for long periods, and without the financial drain of having to subsidise a disgruntled military garrison. In addition to his ancestral holdings in Kent – Brasted, Dacehurst, Edenbridge, Hadlow, Tonbridge and Yalding – he also received at this time, on the death of the Duke of Gloucester, Penshurst and its dependencies, with a magnificent country house. All this, together with control of Dover Castle and the Cinque Ports, and his large stake in the customs at Sandwich (at that time England's busiest port), gave him a substantial degree of control over Kentish affairs. This was particularly important to him with his Lancastrian outlook, as Kent was strongly Yorkist in its sympathies as was demonstrated in Cade's Rebellion. It has been suggested that Stafford initiated the purchase of the Wardenship before resigning from Calais, indicating that it was a carefully planned strategic move on his part.[11]

The Warden of the Cinque Ports was *ipso facto* constable of Dover Castle, and its holder exercised considerable civil, military and naval authority as it combined the functions of sheriff, Custos Rotulorum, Lord Lieutenant and admiral at Dover, Sandwich, Hastings, Romney and Hythe and also Winchelsea, Rye and Lydd. As the

15 Penshurst Place, Kent was inherited by Humphrey, Duke of Buckingham from his father-in-law, the Duke of Gloucester, together with large estates in Kent which augmented the Audley inheritance. (NMR)

Cinque Ports had the obligation to provide and man ships for the King this also in theory gave the Warden control over naval forces.

Stafford appointed Sir Thomas Kyriel (who had worked for him at Calais) as his lieutenant at Dover and the Cinque Ports at an annual salary of £10.[12] His Receiver at Dover was Thomas Hexstell who was also his Receiver for the counties of Kent and Surrey, indicating that he intended to manage the Warden's interests and his territorial estates as a single entity. When the crunch came, however, Stafford's carefully built-up authority proved to be ineffective and Kent, led by his half-brother Archbishop Bourchier of Canterbury, and his neighbour Lord Cobham, joined Edward Duke of York when he landed more or less unopposed at Sandwich in 1459.

After his mother's death in 1438 he was known as Earl of Buckingham, and was created 1st Duke of Buckingham on 14 September 1444. After a contretemps with Henry Beauchamp, the short-lived Duke of Warwick, he secured in 1447 a special grant of precedence before all dukes of subsequent creation except the blood royal. By being made a duke he thus achieved the 'pinnacle of legitimate social ambition'. He took great pride in his position as premier duke of England. Though diligent and hard working and very loyal to the King, contemporaries found him unlikable. There is evidence both in England and France for lack of cordiality towards him. The French, for instance, noted his offensive behaviour during the trial of Joan of Arc. Despite his arrogance and aloofness he seems, however, to have had the streak of serious piety which runs through the family and in his will he asked to be buried simply 'without any sumptuous costes or charges', and left 200 marks to the poor to pray for his soul.

He had close connections with the Church. As has been seen, members of his family occupied with distinction some of the highest offices in the late medieval English hierarchy. As well as his cousin John Stafford, his half-brother Thomas Bourchier also served as Archbishop of Canterbury. The two archbishops filled the role of Primate of England, with only a short breach, for nearly the whole of the period between 1443 and 1486. Archbishop John Stafford, together with the Queen, had been Humphrey's guardian during his minority. Cardinal Beaufort had been an influence on his political development and something of a role-model in his youth. The marriage of Buckingham's eldest son Humphrey to Margaret Beaufort, daughter of the Duke of Somerset, may have been a result of his association with the Cardinal.

In the later Middle Ages, the Stafford family's spiritual life was much influenced by the orders of friars. The Duke of Buckingham's confessor was a friar, Robert Topping from Chelmsford. His principal chaplain, however, was a priest of noble birth, Fr Philip Vater. Buckingham maintained an elaborate liturgy in the chapels of his various houses, with choirs of singing men and boys. He also had control over the religious appointments on his estates which comprised the advowson of 23 parish churches, six priories, three chapels and three chantries. Like his ancestors from Robert de Toeni onwards, he was a patron and benefactor of religious foundations. He endowed a chapel at Stafford, co-founded a chantry guild at Thame, Oxfordshire, established a hermit (to maintain the road between Stokenchurch and Hereford), founded a chantry at St Mary, Writtle (Essex), and gave manors to Eton College, Atherstone Priory, and St Mary the Virgin, Cambridge. In his will he left 100 marks to the college at Maxstoke (to endow an additional canon) and 100 marks invested in land to support perpetually three additional priests at his grandfather's foundation at Pleshey in Essex.[13]

Almost immediately after his ducal promotion he was caught up in the civil war, known as the War of the Roses, when public order in England finally collapsed after years of incompetent rule; and great families, like the Staffords, maintained their power and security by employing indentured retainers or private armies, a system of mutual support known as 'Livery and Maintenance'. To an extent the troubles were provoked by Buckingham's own intervention on behalf of Henry VI whom he provided with a bodyguard. It was at this period that the family adopted the famous Stafford knot as their badge of livery, worn as a sign of allegiance by their followers as well as being emblazoned as a mark of ownership on their own property. The

16 Maxstoke Castle, Warwickshire was the favourite house of Humphrey 1st Duke of Buckingham, who largely rebuilt it.

Stafford's had several badges: another being a flaming cart wheel. Buckingham used them conjoined, as can be seen in the carved stonework of his favourite country house, Maxstoke Castle in Warwickshire, which he largely rebuilt. The Stafford family is supposed to have adopted their knot symbol in the time of Hugh the 2nd Earl, from a Wake ancestor. The knot certainly appears on his wife Joan Wake's seal in the British Museum. It can also be seen embroidered on the chasuble (now in the Victoria and Albert Museum) worn at the wedding of the 5th Earl of Stafford in 1398. It was widely adopted, however, by the 1st Duke and his successors in the 15th century. The Paston letters record that the Duke had 2,000 Stafford knots made at this time as badges of livery for his retainers.

The civil war and collapse of public order after 1450 was brought about by prolonged economic slump following the Black Death in the 14th century, the ignominious collapse of the English conquests in France in the 1440s, and finally the weak personal rule of Henry VI culminating in mental incapacity when his queen, Margaret of Anjou, and her Court adherents drove the Duke of York and his supporters into open rebellion. Humphrey Duke of Buckingham was loyal to Henry VI and in 1454 was wounded in the face defending him during the skirmish in the streets of St Albans where the King was captured by the supporters of Edward, Duke of York. The Duke of Buckingham recovered but his eldest son Humphrey, Earl of Stafford was killed in that fracas.

Buckingham was drawn into the dynastic controversy by his rank and position rather than as a result of strong views or his own positive volition. His pride in his titles and distinctions and connections with the ruling house (his mother was first cousin of Henry V) led him naturally to support the rights of the great feudal nobility and the person of the King, inclinations which had been further ingrained by the example and influence of Cardinal Beaufort who had been the leader of the feudal nobility, temporal and spiritual, in the early years of Henry VI's reign. Buckingham's family connections, however, pulled him back from an extremist position and placed him midway between the two contending factions. The Staffords were closely linked by marriage and descent to the leading Yorkist families such as the Mowbrays, while his half-brothers, the Bourchiers, were strong Yorkists. Despite his own Lancastrian loyalties, he remained on good terms with these Yorkist relations, especially Archibishop Bourchier, as is indicated in their surviving correspondence.[14] This family connection may explain the moderation he displayed throughout the greater part of the struggle. But the English noble families were all so intermixed that blood ties can hardly be used to explain any of the alignments at this time.

There is no doubt, however, that Buckingham was one of the more moderate men who deplored the drift into armed conflict. Though he had maintained a certain aloofness from Suffolk (the Queen's instrument) he had given him passive support. Except when he was at Calais he had attended all the meetings of parliament and the council. When Suffolk was murdered (the event usually taken as the watershed in the affairs of mid-15th-century England) there is little evidence for Stafford's personal reaction to unfolding events. Though his eldest son was married to Margaret Beaufort, daughter of the Duke of Somerset, he did not associate himself with Somerset's bitter attack on the Duke of York. After Somerset's death at St Albans, and the establishment of York's protectorate, Buckingham regularly attended the privy council. The Bourchier brothers were made chancellor and treasurer while the youngest, John, was made a peer as Lord Berners. Buckingham was persuaded by the Yorkists to lend his support and to '… come inn … and draw the lyne with them … and thereto he and his brethren be bounde by reconysaunce in notable summes to abyde the same'.[15]

After Henry VI temporarily recovered in 1456 the Bourchiers were dismissed by the Queen at the parliament at Coventry in the autumn of that year, and York and his supporters were attainted. Buckingham and his family had failed. 'It is said that the Duke of Buk taketh right straungeley that bothe his brethren are so sodeynly discharged from ther offices of Chancellerie and Tresoryship.'[16]

From then on his actions bespeak a sense of despair. He made no effort to prevent the royal troops from sacking Ludlow (a Yorkist stronghold) though he did offer asylum to the Duchess of York. His anger at the dismissal of the Bourchiers was compounded by the French attack on Sandwich, instigated by the Queen, which represented a direct blow to his own financial interests. But he seems to have been fatalistic, and relinquished his strategic control in Sandwich and Kent without effort. While in residence at Maxstoke in 1559 he wrote his will, which can be interpreted as a sign that he had given up hope, and did not expect to live long. He continued to act according to his guiding principle of personal loyalty to the King and joined Henry VI at Northampton in 1460. There the Duke of York and his chief supporters the Earl of Warwick, having marched from Kent, and Archbishop Bourchier, the papal legate, several bishops and many peers, met the royal army. The Bishop of Salisbury was sent by the Yorkists to ask the King to accept mediation by the clergy. This was rejected by Buckingham, as Henry VI's spokesman. Battle was joined and the Yorkists gained an easy victory thanks to the defection to them of Lord Grey of Ruthyn. Buckingham himself was killed without attempting to defend himself. A career which had seemed brilliant and full of promise, beginning with Henry V's victories in France and gilded by a dukedom, ended in disappointment and failure. He was buried, with others who were slain, at the Greyfriars in Northampton.[17]

He was succeeded by his grandson Henry, the eldest son of Humphrey, styled Earl of Stafford (who had died at St Albans), and Margaret Beaufort. Henry's mother was the daughter of Edmund, 2nd Duke of Somerset (the Lancastrian leader also slain at St Albans) and Eleanor Beauchamp, daughter of Richard Earl of Warwick, Edward IV's most powerful supporter. His was therefore an inheritance which straddled the dynastic divide.

Henry, 2nd Duke of Buckingham (1455-1483) was only five years old and a minor when he inherited in 1460. He became the ward of Anne Duchess of Exeter, sister to Edward IV. As a result of her influence he was married to Katherine Wydvill or Woodville, daughter of Earl Rivers and sister of Edward IV's Queen, which made him in due course brother-in-law to the King. The 2nd Duke was created a Knight of the Bath, aged ten, in 1465 at the coronation of Elizabeth Woodville, wife of Edward IV, and was created a Knight of the Garter in 1474.

Duke Henry remains a shadowy figure of whom little is known. He was well educated and politically astute and took an active interest in the management of his large estates. As well as being premier duke he was outstanding for his wealth (after the Duke of York became King as Edward IV, the Stafford-Buckinghams were the richest of English peers) and the extent of his territorial possessions. For a hundred and sixty years, up to the death of his grandfather in 1460, the Staffords had prospered in the service of the Crown; their wealth, lands and illustrious marriages were the result of royal patronage as well as their own personal talents as soldiers and statesmen. They had risen from a local power base in the Midlands to the highest rank of the nobility with large estates spread across England. But now all this changed.[18]

The 2nd Duke received no favours from Edward IV, the relative insecurity of whose throne made him suspicious of the Stafford's royal blood, traditional support for the Lancastrian dynasty which had been unswerving since the revolution of 1399 when Henry IV had taken the throne, and his pre-eminent position and wealth. A combination of frustrated ambition and fear (and possibly dislike of the Woodvilles) led the Duke, on Edward IV's death, to support the claim of Richard of Gloucester to the throne rather than the little Prince Edward who was dispatched to the Tower and never heard of again.

Buckingham's great services to Richard III were rewarded by the new King with grants of important offices including the Wardenship of the Cinque Ports and the hereditary Lord High Constableship of England. This office meant much to the Buckinghams; their right to it came through Lady Anne Plantagenet as part of the Bohun inheritance. The Lord High Constable was one of the Great Offices of State, like the Earl Marshal or the Lord Great Chamberlain, which emerged after the Conquest when the Anglo-Norman court modelled itself on the pattern of Charlemagne's. The office of Lord High Constable had become annexed to the earldom of Hereford and descended for nine generations in the Bohun family. The post had originally been granted by the Empress Maud (daughter of Henry I) to Milo of Gloucester whose daughter Margaret married Humphrey de Bohun, Earl of Hereford. As part of the division of the Bohun estates between Eleanor and Mary, the constableship had gone to Mary who married Henry IV, while the earldoms of Hereford and Northampton passed to Eleanor and the Staffords. The death of Henry VI in 1460 made possible the re-unification of the constableship with the earldom of Hereford in the person of the Duke of Buckingham. Richard III's grant was the confirmation of Duke Henry's cherished claim. The Constable was originally responsible for the Court as a battle horde or army and he presided over the Coronation and other ceremonies. The holding of the ancient office reinforced Duke Henry's position at the head of the peerage of England.[19]

Duke Henry's role had also been buttressed by the prestigious marriages made by his sisters, thanks to the family fortune which enabled them to be endowed with substantial portions. Lady Joan married William son and heir of John Viscount Beaumont (a descendant of the family which had produced the last Christian king of the Latin Kingdom of Jerusalem) in 1452, while Katherine married John Earl of Shrewsbury in 1458. His own mother Margaret Duchess of Buckingham was, as has been seen, the daughter and heiress of the 2nd Duke of Somerset. These marriages strengthened the already formidable inter-connections between the Stafford family and other senior members of the English nobility.

The best-documented aspect of the lives of the 15th-century Dukes of Buckingham is the administration of their estates and household, for which more original papers survive than for any other English medieval family. The Dukes of Buckingham derived most of their income and all their territorial influence from large estates spread over many counties. Efficient management and effective revenue collection alone made it possible for them to maintain an impressive household, and to attract the followers essential for security and reputation. The administration of estates stretching from Dover to Wales, from Hampshire to Holderness was no small task in the 15th century with no speedier means of communication than horseback and the written or spoken word.

The Duke's estates had been built up from their 11th-century nucleus in Staffordshire by a series of successful marriages which had brought lands in various parts of England and shares in the inheritances of several great medieval families, notably the de Clares Earls of Gloucester and the Bohuns Earls of Hereford.

In the 15th century the estates were organised into eight receiverships, each based on a different region with a central castle and administrative system responsible for local management and revenue collection. Above this was a body of trustees, the Lords' Council, which was based in London. Following young Henry's accession after his grandfather's death in battle in 1460 there was a long minority until January 1473 when he came of age. Duchess Anne (Henry's grandmother) had taken possession of her lands (as her jointure under the terms of her marriage settlement) including Holderness in 1461, a year after the death of her husband. She was also given custody of her late husband's other English property and all but two of the Welsh receiverships. The other Welsh receiverships were controlled by the King himself, for political reasons. The family's possession and the established administration of the Buckingham estates was not, therefore, interrupted by the 1st Duke's untimely death, but continued seamlessly, and no problems arose from Duke Henry's long minority. Though the duchess was remarried (to Walter Blount, Lord Mountjoy), she maintained a smaller, more centralised household than her late husband's. This reduced the ducal expenditure and made it easier to control the family finances; so that everything was in good heart by the time Henry took 'livery' of his lands in 1483 on coming of age.[20]

The records for Duke Henry's personal control of the estates between 1473 and 1483 are lost, so his income and debts can only be guessed at. The Welsh Lordships were restored to him in 1473 and Duchess Anne's dower, including the valuable Holderness estate with its large sheep farms, came back to him on her death in 1480. It is likely, however, that his outgoings always exceeded his income, as is indicated by attempts to improve the system of revenue collection in the different receiverships. The Welsh estates always failed to produce their budgeted income for him, as for his predecessors and successor. It was almost certainly his need for royal favours and rewards that encouraged Duke Henry to support Richard of Gloucester's *coup d'état* in 1483.

At first he backed Richard III with enthusiastic loyalty, and performed many important services such as supervising the arrest of Lords Rivers and Grey (the Woodvilles – the unpopular relations of Edward IV's Queen), and taking possession of the children of Edward IV on Richard's behalf. He advised Richard to have the two princes declared illegitimate. In return Richard invested him with great powers in Wales and five English counties. He was given the stewardship of Tutbury, the royal estate next to his own at Stafford. He was recognised as sole heir of the Bohun family. He was made chief justice and chancellor of Wales and constable of the royal castles there, an almost vice-regal position. He seemed loyal to Richard III, and used his powers of oratory to rally the City of London and other forces in the land to Richard's cause. 'He was neither unlearned and of nature marvellously well-spoken,' as Thomas More was later to describe him.

Apart from his gift for public speaking, other aspects of Duke Henry's character can be glimpsed in his support for Richard III and in other people's perceptions of him; his love of magnificence, for instance, and of rich clothes and trappings. He outshone in splendour all the other magnates in Richard III's coronation procession with his jewelled horse trappings emblazoned with the burning cart wheel badge and his numerous retainers bedecked in red and black livery with the Stafford knot. He was appointed Lord Great Chamberlain and carried the King's train at the coronation.

After this public display of support, and inundated with royal favours, his sudden *volte-face* in August 1483, only a month after being acknowledged as Lord High Constable, took his contemporaries by surprise. Without provocation or warning he deserted Richard and declared his support for Henry Tudor and Elizabeth of York, and their claims to the throne. He departed for Wales to raise an army there, and called upon his tenants and followers throughout his English estates to come out against Richard. His motives can only be guessed. It has been suggested that his dramatic switch of allegiance was caused by guilty conscience over Edward V. This assumes that the 'princes in the Tower' were murdered by Richard in summer 1483 but no definite evidence as to the date of the death of Edward V and his brother, nor the perpetrators, has ever been forthcoming. It is one of the intriguing secrets of English history.

Duke Henry, having raised troops in Wales, marched towards England to join his English retainers but was held up at the Severn. The river was in flood and all the crossing places impassable. On 11 October, Richard proclaimed the Duke of Buckingham a traitor and the 'most untrue creature living'. The Duke's Welsh troops lost heart and deserted, leaving him cut off and isolated. He fled in disguise. A reward of £1,000 was put on his head.

The Duke made it to one of his Midlands estates, where he hid in a poor hut or cottage, attended by a retainer Ralph Bannister who brought him food. It is a scene worthy of Walter Scott. The Duke was supposedly given away, by the evidence of his dinner being conveyed to the little hut, which aroused suspicion. Whatever the truth, the seemingly loyal Bannister later claimed the reward for the Duke's discovery. According to legend the Duke was apprehended hiding in an oak chest. He was taken to Salisbury where the Court was in residence. Without legal trial he was there summarily beheaded in the Market Place, aged 28 years, and buried at the Grey Friars. He was attainted as a traitor, and his estates and titles confiscated by the Crown.

Richard III settled an allowance on the Duke's widow Katherine (who subsequently remarried Jasper Tudor), set aside money to pay the Duke's debts, and distributed the larger portion of the Staffords' lands and offices among his own supporters. Far from being a final catastrophe, however, this turned out to be a temporary blip. There was a remarkable turn of fortune. Richard himself had only a short time on the throne before Henry Tudor made good his claim to be King. By marrying Elizabeth of York he united the Lancastrian and Yorkist claims to the throne, thus bringing the Wars of the Roses to an end. Richard was killed at the Battle of Bosworth and Henry VII proclaimed King in 1485. The attainder against the Duke of Buckingham was immediately reversed. His eldest son Edward was restored to all his honours at the age of seven and created a Knight of the Bath on 29 October. All the family estates were restored to him in 1498 on his 20th birthday while technically he was still a minor.

Edward 3rd Duke of Buckingham was to fill the most splendid and most tragic chapter in the history of the Staffords. His royal descent and his wealth made him a dangerous subject. The ambivalent behaviour of his two predecessors gave grounds for suspicion that he might be a potential rebel. His failure to allay these fears was to cause his downfall and terminate both the dukedom and the hereditary office of Lord High Constable of England.

IV

The Tragedy of the Third Duke

❧·❧

EDWARD DUKE OF BUCKINGHAM (1478-1521), Earl of Stafford, Hereford and Northampton, Lord of Brecon and Holderness, was heir general to both Edward III and Henry VI. Following the attainder of the Duke of Norfolk in 1485, he was the only extant English duke. He had an annual income of about £6,000 (gross), by far the largest of any English peer of his time.[1] He and his ancestors had occupied high office under the Crown for centuries as 'councillors of state and captains of arms' including the constableships of England, Calais and France. His estates were the most extensive in the country; his lands spread from Holderness in Yorkshire to Kent. He was the greatest of the Welsh Marcher Lords. He owned houses in Calais and possessed titles to land in France and Ireland. All this was to be lost when he was condemned to death for treason, at the age of forty-three.

Whereas the documentary evidence for his ancestors is meagre, it is copious for Duke Edward; and a more rounded biography is possible than for any of his predecessors. He was a reasonably efficient administrator interested in the management of his estates, an hospitable and generous lord entertaining vast numbers of persons in his various houses, the patron of dramatic players and musicians, a benefactor of learning with a particular interest in Magdalene College Cambridge (which owns his portrait), and supporting poor scholars at Oxford; he was a connoisseur of architecture whose rebuilding of Thornbury Castle in Gloucestershire as his principal seat produced the most magnificent of the early Tudor palaces and, like his predecessors, was a supporter and benefactor of religious institutions. Against this he was arrogant, high-handed, bad-tempered and vindictive towards those whom he thought had crossed him. His love of splendour was carried to conceited excess.

His early childhood had been remarkably adventurous. When his father, the 2nd Duke, had embarked on his insurrection against Richard III he had sent his young son and heir to Weobley in Herefordshire where he was entrusted to the care of a trusted family supporter, Sir Richard Delabeare. Delabeare took the little boy to his own

17 Portrait of Edward, 3rd Duke
of Buckingham, 1520.

home at Kinnersley on the Welsh Border where the child was looked after by a
retainer, William Ap Symon and Delabeare's own wife, Dame Elizabeth. She showed
great courage and resource, disguising the little boy as a girl. There was a reward of
£1,000 on his head, and the Vaughan family (who had been Buckingham retainers but
turned against them) sacked Brecon Castle and led the hunt for the little boy. Search
parties visited Kinnersley twice, but both times Dame Elizabeth successfully hid him
in the woods, before William Ap Symon led him in a daring escape disguised as a
gentlewoman and riding side saddle.[2]

The future 3rd Duke remained in hiding until the accession of Henry VII in 1485.
The attainder against him was reversed at Henry VII's first parliament and Edward
Stafford was restored to all his titles and estates at the age of eight. He was created
a Knight of the Bath at the Coronation and educated in the royal household under
the direction of Lady Margaret Beaufort, the King's mother. The 3rd Duke's life-long

interest in books and education owed much to this upbringing at a Court which was still redolent of the late medieval traditions of piety and chivalry. During his minority his lands were well-managed by his guardians. On coming of age in 1498 he was granted special livery of his lands, but Henry VII charged him £3,000 for the privilege. This rankled with the Duke and alienated him from the King who had in other ways treated him generously. In 1515 the Duke sued Henry VII's executors for recovery of this sum. The judges found against him, but Henry VIII gave him back £1,000 as a mark of special favour in an abortive attempt to win his goodwill. By that date, however, there was a well-developed sense of mistrust on both sides between the Tudors and the Buckinghams.[3]

Immediately after he obtained custody of his entire inheritance in 1498 Duke Edward embarked on sweeping reforms throughout the estates, aimed at raising rents, cutting costs and centralising the administration under his council sitting at Thornbury. Despite his huge land holdings, his actual income fell short of his annual expenditure, and this was exacerbated by his indebtedness to the Crown. Drastic measures were necessary. He made widespread use of litigation, arbitration or naked force to secure his administrative ends. In the course of his life he sued 72 persons for trespass, 45 for theft and 15 for infringement of his rights as a landlord. In his reforming policies he was following in the footsteps of his mother, Lady Margaret, and the trustees during his minority. He was successful in reducing running costs and local administrative expenses. He also increased agricultural production and rental income in varying degrees throughout his English estates and instituted closer supervision in all areas to cut out waste though his policies were partly hampered by the unsatisfactory quality of some of the local officials. Only in the Welsh estates did his reforms make no progress at all and there his actions further unsettled an already lawless region causing serious problems.[4]

All income was sent from the eight receiverships to the Duke's cofferer who was responsible for financing the three principal departments of expenditure: the Wardrobe, the Great Household (at Thornbury) and the Riding Household (when the Duke progressed between his other houses and estates). Altogether he employed 164 officials to administer his estates. Apart from archaic castles all over the country, the Duke had a number of principal houses in different regions, notably Maxstoke Castle in Warwickshire (a moated fortified manor house), Tonbridge Castle (inherited from the Audleys) and Penshurst Place (which had been granted to the 1st Duke in Kent). Smaller houses, such as Stafford Castle, he used as hunting lodges rather than regular residences. Henry VIII's commissioners described Stafford Castle in the 1520s as 'this little castle … standing pleasantly nigh much game for hunting … should be right pleasant for the king when it shall please His Grace to make his progress into those parts.' Its symmetrical 14th-century toy castle architecture seems still to have been admired, however, for it was praised as being 'all uniform and of one fashion'. There were three chambers in each of the five towers, a 'nether hall' on the ground floor,

18 Thornbury Castle, Gloucestershire: the private apartments rebuilt by the 3rd Duke with large bay windows. (NMR)

and a Great Hall and Great Chamber on the first floor hung with tapestry and furnished with stools and benches bearing the Stafford knot.[5] The Duke was keen on hunting, and owned 23 well-stocked deer parks on his estates.

Duke Edward's principal seat was Thornbury Castle, the *caput* of the Gloucestershire estates, inherited (like Tonbridge in Kent) from the Audleys and de Clares. There he lived surrounded by ceremonial magnificence and served by a household of 130 people.[6] The reconstruction of this manor as a semi-fortified country seat was the Duke's greatest architectural project. It was planned around two principal quadrangles flanked by a subsidiary kitchen court and a walled privy garden. The house and dependencies covered an area of 12 acres, equivalent in ground size, if not scale of buildings, to Windsor Castle. The Duke obtained a licence to crenellate in 1510, and Thornbury was a late example of the castle aesthetic, with two tall turretted gate houses and castellations, though the defensive air was offset by huge glazed windows, and myriad ornamental chimneystacks. New building and adaptations of older structures (the great hall was retained as the focus of the principal quadrangle) probably were underway before 1510. Work in earnest began in 1511 with the foundation of the gate-house to the inner quadrangle and over the following years the Duke completed the main part of the house including chapel, state apartments and private chambers, all surrounding a compact inner court with square or octagonal towers at the corners. The old great hall filled the north range with kitchens to the left. The larger outer quadrangle with stables, store rooms and lodgings for the household was still unfinished in 1521, because the project was halted by the Duke in 1519 while he was at Court and away with the King in France. The existing stock of good stone on site had been used up by then, and the Duke, who had never managed to live within his income, was seriously short of money. By 1520 his debts amounted to £10,535.[7]

The Duke's 'new buildings' at Thornbury were among the finest pieces of early Tudor architecture; the great bay windows of the state rooms are comparable to Henry VII's Chapel at Westminster. The Duke's pride in the work is evidenced by the liberal sprinkling of the Stafford knot and his personal motto 'Hence Forward'. Over the entrance is inscribed: 'This gateway was begun in the yere of Our Lorde God 1511, the second yere of the Reign of Kynge Henry VIII by me Edward, Duc of Buckingham, Erle of Hereforde, Staforde, and Northampton.' In addition to the house, the Duke laid out extensive gardens and imparked large areas. The privy garden was bounded by a two-storeyed gallery leading to the adjoining parish church. The Duke's privy garden was described as a 'goodly garden to walk in, closed with high walls and embattled'. This is still a major feature of Thornbury today. There were also a 'large and goodly orchard', rose arbours, and pleached walks with seats. Further away from the castle were three parks containing 1,550 fallow and red deer: Marlwood Park, Eastwood Park, and the Duke's 'New Park' which he formed by enclosing 1,200 acres. This was not without controversy, as it was claimed that some of the land was copyhold and the tenants had not received due compensation. The Duke's enclosures were unpopular, here for deer, but elsewhere for sheep, and an example of his high-handed and overbearing conduct.[8]

The Duke also intended to transform the church at Thornbury into a grand collegiate establishment and obtained a licence for this in 1514. Ecclesiastical colleges were a characteristic feature of the capital of a great feudal lord in the late Middle Ages, as can be seen at Tattershall in Lincolnshire, for instance, where Ralph, Lord Cromwell rebuilt the castle and founded a collegiate church in the 15th century. The Duke of Buckingham's College at Thornbury was to be on a characteristically grand scale with a choir of 18 men and nine boys, which compares, for example, with the Earl of Arundel's collegiate establishment of eight men and four choir boys at Arundel.[9]

By the standards of the time the Duke was a pious man. He attended daily Mass, gave alms widely, and regularly went on pilgrimages to shrines and religious houses, especially at Easter time. Like his medieval ancestors he was a generous benefactor of churches and religious bodies. He gave land worth £60 p.a. to Tewkesbury Abbey in Gloucestershire, £20 towards the cost of completing the stone vault at St George's Chapel, Windsor, an endowment of £300 p.a. for his new college at Thornbury and

19 Thornbury Church, reconstructed by the 3rd Duke as an ambitious collegiate establishment. (NMR)

rebuilt parts of other Gloucestershire churches. Eastington church, for instance, is decorated with his four heraldic badges carved in stone in commemoration of his munificence.[10]

'Bounteous Buckingham, the mirror of courtesy' is remembered as a great lord entertaining on a medieval scale at Thornbury. This is partly because of the survival of some of the contemporary accounts and the *Stafford Household Book* which was published by the Society of Antiquaries in 1838. Vast quantities of food were consumed, not just by the Duke's family and household (amounting to about 130 people), but by a private army of liveried retainers, visiting gentry and clergy, beggars and minstrels (Thornbury also boasted a fool and a dancing bear). On an ordinary day the Duke, his family, guests, and servants consumed 220 loaves of bread, nine quarts of Gascon

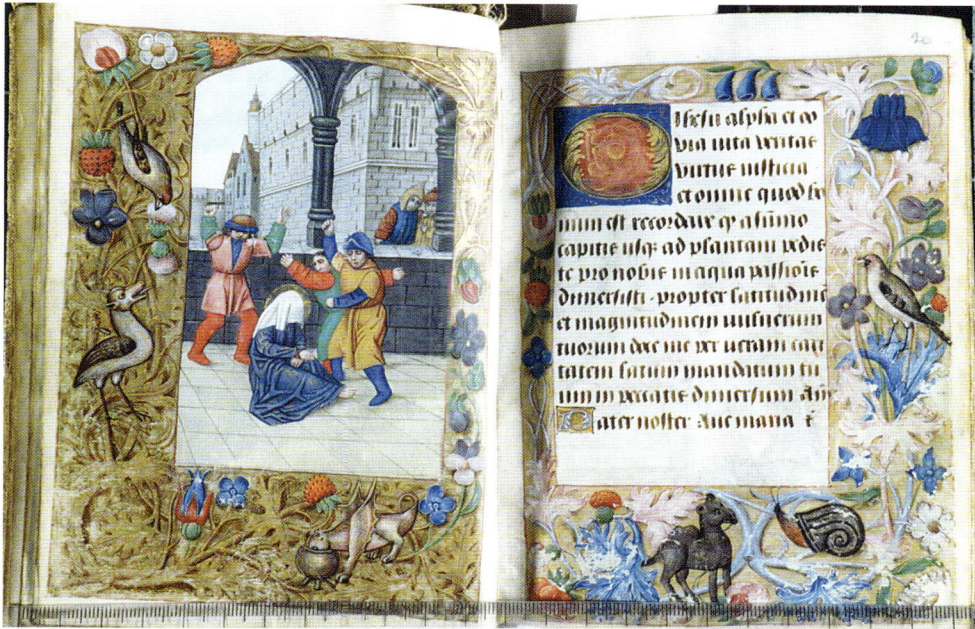

20 Stafford Prayer Book: illuminated Book of Hours from the library at Thornbury. (Arundel Castle)

wine (claret), 81 flagons of beer, 12 rounds of beef, four sheep, half a deer, half a pig, two geese, two suckling pigs, three capons, seven rabbits, three woodocks, one mallard, six swans, eight lambs, 60 eggs and four dishes of butter.[11] Even more lavish entertainment took place at the castle on the great feasts of the year. On Christmas Day 1509, for instance, the Duke provided dinner for 95 gentry, 107 yeomen, 97 grooms; and supper for 84 gentry, 105 yeomen and 92 grooms. On the feast of the Epiphany there dined at Thornbury 134 gentry, 176 valets or yeomen and 98 grooms. Consumption rose to 678 loaves of bread, eight gallons of wine, 245 flagons of beer, peacocks, sturgeon, lampreys and 200 oysters as well as the usual swans, beef, sheep and game.[12] Entertainment was supplied by four players, two minstrels, six trumpeters and four 'waits'. High Mass was sung in the chapel by the Abbot of Kingswood and six of his monks, assisted by the Duke's chaplain and the choir of 18 men and nine boys.[13]

Such splendid hospitality was expected of the Duke and was an essential aspect of his status. His grandeur was also reflected in his fabulous clothes and jewels, and by his gold and silver plate which was valued at £2,494 in 1520.[14] Everything in his daily life was splendid. An indication remains in his superb French illuminated 'Book of Hours' which is preserved in the library at Arundel Castle. The Duke's love of magnificence was part grounded in a feeling for history and concern for his ancestors. This historical interest in his own family was also connected with the administration of the estates, as he used his archives for litigation purposes in the constant lawsuits in which he engaged against neighbours, tenants, employees and debtors. He began to classify his family papers and stored them together with copies of his own papers and accounts in 'ironbound chests with locks and bolts' in a specially built Muniment Room on the top floor of a tower in the inner court at Thornbury.

His officials at the eight different receiverships were instructed to sort and send their historical papers to Thornbury for safekeeping. This is one reason why so much of the Stafford-Buckingham estate archive still survives today, despite the vicissitudes of the intervening centuries.[15] Like many of the late medieval and Tudor nobility, the Duke's education had included Law, in which he took a keen interest. His own reading included such legal tomes as Littleton's *Tenures* and works on statute law. He liked to engage in discussion with clever legal minds as a form of recreation. He also bought books and supported scholars at Oxford and Cambridge. Wynkyn de Worde in 1512 printed an edition of *The History of Helyas, Knight of the Swan* at the Duke's instigation.[16]

Though restored to his titles and lands by Henry VII, he was employed by the King chiefly for ceremonial duties rather than being entrusted with any great business of state, or admitted to the council. Henry VII was distrustful of the great magnates like Buckingham whom he saw as a potential threat to the Crown. The Tudor monarchs followed a consistent policy of reducing the independent power of the nobility and transforming nobles into courtiers and servants of the Crown restricted to military and ceremonial roles rather than co-participants in the exercise of political power. The Duke of Buckingham took part in the pageants at Court in 1494 when Prince Henry, the King's second son, was created Duke of York, and the following year he was made a Knight of the Garter. In 1497 he was appointed Captain of the royal army dispatched to suppress the Cornish rebels. In 1501, the year after his marriage to Alianora Percy, daughter of Henry, 4th Earl of Northumberland, he was sent to meet Catharine of Aragon and convey her to London for her marriage to Prince Arthur, the heir to the throne. On 9 March 1503/4 he acted as High Steward at the enthronement of Archbishop Warham of Canterbury. On such occasions the Duke dressed magnificently in cloth of gold trimmed with sable, and fulfilled his role appropriately.

With the accession of the young King Henry VIII in 1508, prospects seemed to look brighter for Buckingham. He was appointed Lord High Constable and Lord High Steward for Henry VIII's coronation at Westminster Abbey on 23 June 1509. He also carried the crown on that occasion. In November he was admitted to the Privy Council. It soon became apparent, however, that Henry VIII shared his father's distrust of the feudal magnates. As his personal companions the new King liked to be surrounded by his contemporaries, energetic young men who shared his sporting interests, while the day-to-day government was entrusted to a series of non-noble but brilliant administrators such as Cardinal Wolsey. 'There was no room in Henry VIII's conception of the monarchy for peers who thought of themselves as the King's equals, assumed they had an inherent right to political power and royal patronage, or obstructed the implementation of Tudor policy in the regions they dominated.'[17] His misunderstanding of Henry VIII was to be the chief reason for the Duke's downfall.

To the Duke of Buckingham, at the beginning of the reign, there seemed to be scope for emulating the military achievements of his ancestors. Henry VIII as a young king had a great ambition to regain the lost English possessions in France and to continue the warlike policies of his Plantagenet and Lancastrian predecessors, especially those of his namesake, Henry V. Over the years vast sums of money were spent on military campaigns in northern France, the net effect of which was nil. The first big French expedition was from June to October 1513. The Duke took part as Captain of the English Army, with 800 of his own men. He commanded the right wing at Therouanne. The campaign, which involved the siege of a few French towns, resulted in a truce and was considered a success, though the major military triumph of the Tudor age took place while the King, his chief minister Cardinal Wolsey, the Duke of Buckingham and the royal army were all out of the country, when Thomas Howard, Earl of Surrey (2nd Duke of Norfolk) annihilated the Scots at Flodden.

At this stage in the reign, Buckingham considered himself to be high in the King's favour. In August 1519 he spent £1,550 in entertaining Henry VIII at Penshurst with dazzling splendour, an event which eerily presaged Cardinal Wolsey's fate at Hampton Court, or the French minister, Fouquet's entertainment of Louis XIV at Vaux le Vicomte a century and a half later, where the grandeur of the entertainment instead

21 Portrait by Hans Holbein of Thomas Howard, 3rd Duke of Norfolk, who married the daughter of the 3rd Duke of Buckingham. (Arundel Castle)

of pleasing the Sovereign stimulated bitter jealousy. Henry VIII, already nursing the traditional wariness of the King towards the over-mighty Buckinghams, now added to this basic political antagonism a poisonous personal rivalry. The Duke himself seems to have been blithely unaware of his danger and made no effort to allay kingly suspicion by the playing down of his own royal connections or cutting back on vain-glorious personal display. This is shown in the grandiose marriages he arranged for his children to other noble families with royal connections. His son and heir, Henry Lord Stafford was married to Ursula Pole, the daughter of Margaret Countess of Salisbury (who was herself to end up on the scaffold because of her Plantagenet blood). His eldest daughter Elizabeth was married to Thomas, Earl of Surrey (later 3rd Duke of Norfolk), a descendant of Edward I, whose son Henry (a godson of the King) was to be beheaded by Henry VIII for quartering the royal arms; Katherine the second daughter was married to the Earl of Westmorland, and Mary the youngest to George, 5th Lord Bergavenny in June 1519, two months before the fatal visit of Henry VIII to Penshurst. Both Westmorland and Bergavenny were descended from John of Gaunt, Duke of Lancaster through the marriage of the 1st Earl of Westmorland to Joan, John of Gaunt's daughter. In the circumstances, Buckingham would have been wise to choose spouses for his children from families less close to the throne.

The deterioration of Henry VIII from the slim, handsome, warlike young king to the bloated, jealous, blood thirsty monster he became in old age is an interesting psychological study. The turning point came in about 1520 and was caused by his failure to produce a male heir. This made him particularly sensitive to the behaviour of those among the nobility with royal blood and a possible claim to the throne, especially Buckingham who was next in line if Princess Mary failed to succeed as Queen. The King came to harbour doubts about the Duke's loyalty and to fear that he was aiming at the throne itself.

The Duke of Buckingham compounded the error of the showy Penshurst entertainment the following year, in June 1520, when he and his son Henry Lord Stafford accompanied the King and Wolsey to meet Francis I at the Field of the Cloth of Gold in France. The magnificence of the occasion is legendary. The Duke who was prominent in his role as Lord High Constable spared no expense in kitting out himself and his retinue with rich new robes, gilded armour and jewelled trappings at a cost of nearly £3,000, a sum equal to the whole annual revenue of most leading peers.

This ostentatious show was exacerbated by the Duke's outbursts of temper, in which he said things which would have been better unsaid and which were capable of upsetting the great. On one occasion Wolsey felt it necessary to issue a tactful reprimand. The Duke was an outspoken critic of Wolsey and his policies, and the Tudor exclusion of the nobility from political power.

Little things intersect with great things, and on his way to France the Duke had unwittingly made one enemy too many among his own staff. At Tonbridge Castle he expressed his disapprobation of his steward there, Charles Knyvett, and sacked him for incompetence. Knyvett determined to revenge himself on his master by reporting to the authorities the Duke's 'hot and indiscreet words'.[18] There is no doubt that the Duke could be hard and vindictive in his treatment of underlings, as part of the great drive towards efficiency and profitability.

There are several documented examples of his ill-treatment and persecution of officials whom he suspected had cheated him. He accused his former secretary John Russell of embezzlement. The case was submitted to private arbitration. When this failed to produce the result the Duke wanted, he seized Russell's estates. Russell appealed to the Star Chamber which brought the matter to a higher authority. Higher authority obviously had no doubts about Russell's ability and honesty, as he was subsequently employed at Court.

On another occasion the Duke of Buckingham imprisoned his auditor, John St George, in Gloucester Castle. Again St George appealed to the Crown and was released by royal writ. The Duke confiscated the possessions of a lady-in-waiting Jane Knyvett for some misdemeanour, which infuriated her kinsman Charles Knyvett and gave him added grounds for testifying against the Duke. Another lady-in-waiting, Margaret Gedding (possibly the Duke's mistress), also revenged herself against the Duke by providing Wolsey with hostile evidence.

All the witnesses against the Duke at his trial were his own employees, including the key figures, Robert Gilbert and Edmund Dellacourt. Between 1507 and 1519 Buckingham sued three of his treasurers, three receivers general, two wardrobers, one

22 Magdalene College Cambridge: the hall built at the expense of the 3rd Duke of Buckingham. (NMR)

of his almoners, and the keeper of his jewels over what he deemed to be breaches of their contracts of employment. Most of these 'crimes' were comparatively minor and involved inefficiency rather than theft.[19]

The Duke was high-handed, arrogant and considered himself above the law. He was uncompromising and remorseless in his treatment of people from all ranks of society. He behaved with an obsessive determination to get his own way, as people sometimes do who have a high opinion of their own abilities, privileges and position and a less high one of other people's competence and honesty. Apart from turning his own household into a 'hotbed of fear and suspicion', the Duke's attitude and behaviour had an unsettling impact on the areas around his estates, especially in his Welsh Lordships where his treatment of the inhabitants often ran contrary to royal proclamations. The Tudors and their ministers came to see the Duke as a disruptive force, exacerbating the already low levels of law and order in the Welsh Marches, where effective government depended on close co-operation between great landowners, like Buckingham, and the Crown.

As early as 1499 he had sued Sir Thomas Lucas, Henry VII's solicitor general, over two wardships and this became a long-running private vendetta. After an inconclusive hearing in the Court of the King's Bench, the Duke had taken matters into his own hands by seizing two of Lucas's Norfolk manors. In 1512 he additionally sued Lucas for slander, while Lucas responded by accusing the Duke of suborning witnesses and having 'no more conscience than a dogge'. This long-running feud ended in an appeal by the Duke to the Court of the Star Chamber in London. Buckingham seems to have been unaware of the consequences of bringing this disreputable saga to the notice of the ministers of the Crown. It may have acted as 'the *coup de grace* to his already unenviable reputation'.[20]

Powerful neighbours, alienated by pointless feuds, fearful and disgruntled employees, and whole districts unsettled by high handed acts were the background to the Duke's sudden and dramatic fall which made so great an impact on his contemporaries, and was to be immortalised by Tudor writers and historians: Polydore Vergil, Holinshed, Sir Thomas More and not least Shakespeare in his play *Henry VIII*. Dramatic as Shakespeare's account is, it contains several historical inaccuracies. There is no evidence that the Duke owed his 'come-uppance' to a personal vendetta by Wolsey, the venom-mouthed 'butcher's cur' who supposedly resented the Duke's conceited treatment of an upstart parvenu like himself. Wolsey was aware, however, of the Duke's attitude towards himself, and of the King's distrust of the Duke. At the official reception of the Emperor Charles V at Canterbury in 1520 the Duke had not disguised his irritation at having to extend the silver ewer and basin to Wolsey to wash his hands, as well as to the King and Emperor. Thus derived the amusing apocryphal story of the Cardinal washing his hands in the silver basin, and being rewarded by having the water poured all over his feet by the Duke.

Henry VIII had reason enough himself to want to destroy the Duke, and needed no assistance or extra encouragement from Wolsey. The King took a personal interest in the accusations of treason against Buckingham and interviewed the witnesses himself. Buckingham's ultimate error of judgement was asking for permission to raise a private army to subjugate the Welsh Marshes, which immediately raised memories of his father's revolt against Richard III. Blithely unaware of the gathering storm, Buckingham, after returning to England from the Field of the Cloth of Gold, spent the winter at Thornbury where he occupied his time in estate management, litigation, gardening, his horses, the liturgy in his chapel, music, poetry, and players. He ordered gold cups for the King and Wolsey and a gold pomander for the Queen as New Year gifts in 1521; so was either unaware of the true feelings in regard to himself at Court, or hoped to assuage them?

On 8 April 1521 the Duke was summoned to London. On arrival he was arrested and put in the Tower. His trial for treason took place in Westminster Hall in May before his peers and was presided over by his father-in-law the 2nd Duke of Norfolk who acted as High Steward for the occasion. He was condemned on the deposition of his former employees Delacourt, Gilbert and Knyvett whom he was not allowed to cross-examine. They claimed that he had spoken treason against the King, had listened to prophecies of Henry's death, and entertained a notion of his own right to the Crown as the descendant and representative of Thomas Duke of Gloucester, son of Edward III. Ten years earlier they had heard him utter seditious expressions, 'hot and indiscreet words', concerning the succession to the Crown in the event of the King dying without male issue. This was enough, and the expected verdict was forthcoming, the court having been assured by the King's lawyers that such words were High Treason.

The Duke was beheaded on Tower Hill on 17 May 1521 and buried at the Austin Friars in the City. He was attainted by Act of Parliament in 1523, all his honours declared void and the estates confiscated by the Crown. He was degraded from the Order of the Garter in a quaint game of football whereby Garter King of Arms and Somerset Herald kicked his banner, crest and sword out of St George's Chapel and into the Windsor Castle ditch. In the unexceptional words of the *Dictionary of National Biography* Buckingham was 'certainly guilty of no crimes sufficient to justify his attainder'.[21]

> My life is spann'd already:
>> I am the shadow of poor Buckingham
>> Whose figure even this instant cloud puts on
>> By darkening my clear sun. My Lord farewell.
>
> Shakespeare, *Henry VIII*

V

From Dukes to Shoemakers

❧·❧

D OWNWARD SOCIAL MOBILITY is much less well-documented than its opposite, for the obvious reason that those who have risen in the world are in a position to write about their history, whereas those who have sunk into obscurity are generally lost to sight. The Staffords in their last years, however, are a graphic illustration of decline. They began the 16th century as dukes, but the last male Stafford died in obscurity in 1640, his sister married to a joiner and their son a cobbler in Newport, Shropshire. Thereafter the line goes cold, but there may still be descendants through them of the great medieval houses of Stafford and Bohun and de Clare.

Following the execution and attainder of the 3rd Duke of Buckingham, the hereditary Lord High Constableship of England ceased to exist, future Lord High Constables being appointed only for the day of the coronation. All the estates were confiscated by the Crown. Henry VIII made no fewer than 72 grants out of this windfall to favoured courtiers, supporters and followers.[1] This judicious re-distribution of land helped to stifle any criticism of the Duke's treatment. The King kept the Marcher Lordships in his own hands. Thornbury Castle remained unfinished and remains so to this day, to recall the Duke's premature and dramatic end.

Henry Stafford, the only son and heir of the Duke by Alianore Percy, daughter of the 4th Earl of Northumberland, was left with only the Staffordshire lands and Caus in Shropshire, but, after ten years, on 15 July 1531 the King also allowed him the castle, demesnes and manor at Stafford. Edward VI went further and in 1547 restored him in blood, re-granting him the barony as 1st Lord Stafford of a new creation, but not the dukedom. Queen Mary later also gave him back Thornbury Castle and lands in Gloucestershire as a reward for his service to the Crown in the rebellion of the late Duke of Northumberland. In 1557/8 the House of Lords restored his precedency as a baron to that of his medieval ancestors. If Henry Lord Stafford pondered the fate of his family, he must have been struck by its singularly tragic fate, both his father and

23 Arms of Edward, Lord Stafford, 1613. (College of Arms)

grandfather beheaded and his great-grandfather, great-great-grandfather and great-great-great-grandfather all slain in the Wars of the Roses.[2] Perhaps he was mercifully not given to introspection.

A trait he shared with his father, however, and for him it must have had a sombre tinge, was the interest in the family's past history and inheritances. He continued the last duke's system for preserving the estate records. He made transcriptions and detailed lists of evidence concerning the family estates and titles. These notes were bound up in two cartularies – the Old Cartulary and the New or Great Cartulary – which still survive (in the Staffordshire Record Office). This work of sorting the archives was also continued by his son Henry, 2nd Lord Stafford, who compiled a register *De Rebus Diversis.*[3]

Henry Stafford was one of the best educated members of the Tudor peerage. He had attended both Oxford and Cambridge Universities, and enrolled at Gray's Inn. He mastered Latin and French completely. Throughout his life he developed his learned interests. He composed the epitaph to his unhappy sister Elizabeth (the estranged wife of the 3rd Duke of Norfolk): 'Thou was to me both far and near. A mother, sister, a friend most dear.'[4] Henry Stafford was of a literary and scholarly turn of mind and, as well as sorting the family records, he spent his time writing and translating works from French and Latin to English including two epistles of Erasmus, and a French treatise on forestry. He created the finest private library of his time in England. In 1556 it comprised 350 printed books and manuscripts.[5] Lord and Lady Stafford's 'Household Book' (MS 1546) is preserved in the library at Arundel Castle.

In 1532 Henry Stafford was offered a Knighthood of the Bath by Henry VIII. He declined the honour, preferring to pay a fine of £20. In the 1530s he lived mainly at Stafford Castle, but then it was let for a time to William Rowley for £28 p.a., though Henry Stafford was back in residence by 1546. He became Chamberlain of the Exchequer and Lord Lieutenant of Staffordshire in the 1550s. He actively supported the Commissioners for Dissolution of the Monasteries in the Midlands. Perhaps he was looking in that direction for lands to recompense him for his losses. His religious views are as inscrutable as everything else about him. He changed with the current wind, which was perhaps wise in the circumstances, though he seems to have had some genuine Protestant sympathies at least in his early years. On 2 October 1538 he wrote from Stafford to Henry VIII's new minister (Wolsey's successor), Thomas Cromwell, that he had removed 'the idol called of ignorant persons Saint Erasmus' and had 'so used it that no man shall thereby offend in idolatry hereafter'.[6]

When Henry VIII died, and Edward VI ascended the throne, Stafford curried favour with the strongly Protestant Protector Somerset; and his translation, published

24 Lord Stafford's Household Book. (Arundel Castle)

in 1548, of Fox's *De Vera Differentia Regiae Potestatis et Ecclesiae* (1534) was fulsomely dedicated to the Duke of Somerset. In that, Stafford compared the English Reformation to Solomon's completion of the Temple of David in Jerusalem. During the reign of Edward VI he attended regularly at Court. That his friendship for Somerset was calculated and not disinterested is shown by the fact that, when Somerset in turn was toppled and tried for treason in December 1551, Stafford was one of the peers who tried and condemned him.

The accession of Queen Mary, and the restoration of the Catholic church in England, brought him closer to the Crown and, as has been stated, he was rewarded for his loyalty to the new Queen with the restoration of some of the Gloucestershire estates. Cardinal Pole, the new Archbishop of Canterbury, was his brother-in-law. At this time Stafford published his translations of the two epistles of Erasmus, which were strongly anti-Lutheran in tone. In the next reign Elizabeth made him Lord Lieutenant of Staffordshire; but his religious views seem to have remained more sympathetic to Catholicism and he disassociated himself from the Act of Uniformity. This suggests that he intended to adhere to the Catholic faith, but this was not to be tested, for he died at Caus Castle on 30 April 1563.

He and his wife Ursula, daughter of Sir Richard Pole KG, had a very large family; seven boys and seven girls. Several died in infancy including the eldest son. The second son, Henry, inherited as 2nd Lord Stafford but died at Stafford Castle in 1566 to be succeeded in turn by his brother Edward who lived till 1603.[7] He in turn again was succeeded as 4th Lord Stafford by his eldest surviving son, Edward, who died in 1625. His only son Edward predeceased him, and the barony passed to his grandson Henry who was born in 1625 but died unmarried in 1637. He was a Catholic and 'met death like an angel', so George Conn (the papal agent in London) informed Cardinal Barberini in Rome.[8]

Edward, 3rd Lord Stafford, entertained Queen Elizabeth to dinner at Stafford Castle on her visit to Stafford in August 1575, which stretched his finances. He was described by a contemporary as a 'wasteful man'. He and his son Edward could never make their income match their expenditure. Gradually, the outlying estates in Staffordshire were sold to pay debts until only Stafford Castle and its surrounding lands remained. The younger Edward was said by his steward to have borrowed from 'all men as well as noblemen and gentlemen as any countryman even two shillings or half a crown'. The deer in the castle parks were killed and the land was leased out. In 1610 Stafford Castle was seized by the King as security for Lord Stafford's debts, but he borrowed money from his steward to buy back some of the leases and his wife Isobel used her own money to restock the land. She continued to live at the Castle after her husband's death, until the Civil War in 1643.[9]

These Elizabethan and Jacobean Lords Stafford lived quietly, partly in London, partly at Stafford, fulfilling the duties of their rank. While the heads of the Stafford family led relatively uneventful lives, the same cannot be said for some of their siblings, who spanned a spectrum which embraced diplomacy, scholarly writing, treason, plots and rebellion.[10]

A younger son of Henry, 1st Lord Stafford and Ursula Pole, was Thomas Stafford (1531-1557). He was a condemned rebel and traitor who could have stepped straight from the pages of a Victorian melodrama. Thomas came to a bad end and was executed on Tower Hill aged twenty-six. He was among the first Englishmen to travel widely in his late teens on the Continent as a form of Grand Tour after the completion of his English education. He visited Rome with an introduction from his uncle, Cardinal Pole (who at one stage was considered a possible candidate for the papacy), and stayed in Italy for three years, going on to Venice from Rome. From northern Italy he travelled to Poland, where he stayed for a time at the court of King Sigismund Augustus. At Thomas's behest the Polish king wrote to Queen Mary of England urging her to restore Thomas (not his eldest brother) to the dukedom of Buckingham, as his rightful inheritance. This irregular suggestion from an unusual source was, not surprisingly, ignored. The disappointment, however, helped to unhinge Thomas's judgement.

From Poland he returned to England where he strenuously opposed the Spanish alliance – Queen Mary's marriage to Philip II – and was involved in Suffolk's attempted rebellion against Queen Mary. He was incarcerated briefly in the Fleet Prison, but no serious charges were brought against him and he was fined without being brought to trial. He immediately fled to France where he became a general trouble-maker. When he attempted to call on his uncle, Reginald Pole, who was then at Fontainebleau, the cardinal refused to see him for fear of upsetting Queen Mary. He had become an embarrassment to his family.

Northern France and the Low Countries were full of a ragtag of English Protestants and exiles and other disgruntled English emigrés from Queen Mary's kingdom. Thomas became involved in the intrigues and plots of these groups. His distinguished ancestry and royal descent fuelled his megalomania and he convinced himself that he was the rightful heir to the throne – the very treason for which his grandfather had been unjustly accused, condemned and executed. He started using the full royal arms of England only on his seal, rather than the Stafford arms with a royal quartering, which was tantamount to a claim to the throne. His royal pretensions led to quarrels with other exiles and plotters; nevertheless, he was able to gather round him a small group of followers and backers from among the ranks of the disaffected.

In 1557 he sailed for England with two ships, to make good his claim to the throne. He landed in Yorkshire and captured Scarborough Castle where the unsuspecting garrison did not put up much resistance. The local militia was called out and marched on Scarborough under the command of the 5th Earl of Westmorland (Thomas's uncle by marriage). He was captured and sent to London where he was tried for treason and condemned to be hanged, drawn and quartered. Usually, when a rebel was of noble blood, this grisly sentence was commuted to mere beheading. Thomas was beheaded on Tower Hill on 28 May 1557.[11]

The 16th-century Staffords had a strain of discontent about them and an inclination towards plots against the throne. Another descendant of the Duke of Buckingham who fell foul of the Tudors – though not fatally so – was William Stafford (1554-1612). His mother Dorothy was a daughter of Henry 1st Lord Stafford. (William's parents were Stafford cousins.) He was a precocious scholar and writer, and a benefactor of New College, Oxford. Educated at Winchester and New College, he was appointed a Fellow of New College in 1573 at the age of nineteen. Perhaps not surprisingly, he spent more time away from than in residence at Oxford, and in 1575 he was deprived for 'absenteeism'. He did not hold a grudge against his old college for this treatment and later in life gave valuable books to the library of New College.

His mother, Lady Stafford, was Mistress of the Robes to Queen Elizabeth I and William was drawn by the glittering life of the court. But once there he fell out with the Earl of Leicester, the Queen's favourite, and sulked around the palace till he earned a reputation as a 'lewd, miscontented, young person'.[12] When his brother Sir Edward Stafford was appointed Ambassador to Paris in 1585, William visited him there. On his return to London he sank back to his skulking behaviour and was suspected of involvement in a plot to depose Queen Elizabeth and put Mary Queen of Scots on the throne in her place. Mary was to lose her head as a result, for she was considered by Burghley and the Queen's councillors to be too dangerous to live, and was beheaded at Fotheringhay. Edward, 3rd Lord Stafford, was among the 24 nobles who presided over the trial of Mary Queen of Scots at Fotheringhay in October 1586.[13]

William Stafford was imprisoned in the Tower in 1587 and 1588, but not condemned as a traitor because of lack of evidence. He had learnt a lesson. After his release, he settled down and married in 1593, his wife being Anne Goyne of Norfolk. He returned to the safer world of writing and scholarship and lived quietly in the country for the rest of his life, dying peacefully in his bed in 1612.

The most interesting and enigmatic of the 16th-century Staffords was Sir Edward Stafford, English ambassador in France from 1583 to 1590. This tricky, possibly double-dealing, character left behind him an unsolved mystery. Most contemporaries such as Lord Burghley valued him as a stout champion of England's interests but others such as Walsingham (who ran Queen Elizabeth's 'secret service') suspected him of double-dealing and selling valuable secrets to Spain and other English enemies. The facts of his career are not in doubt, but the interpretation to be placed on them is open to different readings. Edward, too, was a son of Sir William and Dorothy Stafford and married as his second wife a sister of Lord Howard of Effingham. He was among a group of court families who disliked the Earl of Leicester and Leicester's support for the Protestant cause, and who nursed secret Catholic sympathies.

Edward Stafford entered Elizabeth's service as special envoy to France *vis-à-vis* the negotiations for a French marriage. Both Stafford and his mentor, Lord Burghley, favoured a French marriage for Elizabeth. He was employed on that business for four years and it amounted to a training in diplomacy. While in France he fell into extravagant habits, especially a love of gaming, where he lost 6 or 7,000 crowns and got seriously into debt. In September 1583 he was appointed English ambassador to France by Walsingham, in succession to Lord Cobham who wished to come home. Paris was full of English Catholic refugees and agents of Mary Queen of Scots including her ambassador, the Archbishop of Glasgow and Thomas Morgan, her chief partisan. They approached Stafford, whose secretary started to pass them information and told them that Stafford feared for Mary's life.

Walsingham got wind of this and in 1585 sent Thomas Rogers (one of his spies) to Paris to see what Stafford was up to. Rogers, in a letter to Walsingham, accused the ambassador of being on confidential terms with the Catholics and forwarding papists' letters to England, and that he was being bribed by the Duke of Guise. At the same time, the Spanish Ambassador, Bernardino de Mendoza, reported to Philip II that he had good reason to think that Stafford could be bribed to provide information for the King of Spain. He had large debts and needed money. Mendoza wrote in 1586 that the Duke of Guise 'assures me … the English ambassador was needy and he … had given him 3,000 crowns.' This letter (in the Spanish State Papers) seems to corroborate Rogers' information to Walsingham.

In January 1587 Mendoza informed Philip II that the King of Navarre (England's ally) had complained to Elizabeth I that Stafford was supplying secret information to the Duke of Guise. Stafford was furious about this and in retaliation had offered to help Spain: 'This ambassador is much pressed for money, and even if he had not made such an offer as this, his poverty is reason enough to expect from him any service if he thought it was to be renumerated.' On 27 February 1587 Philip II offered Stafford 2,000 crowns to supply news from his own dispatches, especially about English naval preparations against Spain. (Since 1585 England and Spain had been virtually at war; Drake's expedition against Cadiz took place in 1584, and the Armada sailed in 1588.) Mendoza referred to Stafford as 'Julio' or 'The new confidant' in his correspondence home. There is also evidence that, as well as taking bribes and supplying information to the French and Spanish, Stafford misappropriated public funds. Money sent by Elizabeth to the ambassador to pay the supporters of Henry of Navarre was spent by Stafford himself.

It has been suggested that Stafford was bamboozling Mendoza and Guise, and may have been engaged in double secret diplomacy in order to ascertain what Spain was up to, and to monitor the activities of the English Catholic refugees in Paris. The evidence he supplied to Mendoza about the Cadiz expedition was accurate, however; he needed money, and personally disliked the Earl of Leicester and Henry of Navarre. The reports in the Spanish State Papers are unequivocal; Walsingham distrusted him. It is impossible to say whether he was consciously or intentionally a traitor, but it seems likely that he was. His dubious activities, however, never caught up with him in England. He returned to London in 1589 but was sent back to France the following year on a mission to the French Protestant leader Henry of Navarre. He finally retired in 1590 and died peacefully and undisturbed in England in 1605. In the words of Conyers Read, 'We know what he did, but we can only guess at what he intended.'[14]

The last Lords Stafford mainly lived quietly in the country, Catholics on dwindling estates. Stafford Castle was considered very old-fashioned and ill-kempt by this time; Edward 3rd Lord Stafford referred to it as his 'rotten castle of Stafford' in a letter to Lord Shrewsbury in July 1603, though both he and his successor spent time there. Edward 3rd Lord Stafford is perhaps best remembered for his exchange with Richard

Bagot of Blithfield over the origins of their family. Stafford wrote to Richard Bagot in terms of high indignation:

> The High Shereef of this shyre lately told me that you pretend my name to be Bagot, and not Stafford, which untrew speeches you have said unto dyvers others, although som dronken ignorant herawld, by you corrupted therein, has soothed your lying, I do therefor answer you that I do better know the descents and matches of my own lyneage than any creature can informe me; for in all my records, pedigrees and armes, from the first Lord Stafford, that was possessed of this castle afore the Conquest, bearing the very same coate I now do, *the feeld Gould, a Chevron Gules,* I cannot find that any Stafford married with a Bagot, or they with him. I have faire recorde to prove that the Lords of my hows were never without heirs male to succed one after another, and therefor your pretens in alledginge that Bagot married an ancester's wief of mine (as per-adventure she married her servant), yet will I prove that neither she, nor no wydow of my hows did take a second husband before they were grandmothers by the children of their first husband; and therefor the lady of my hows was too old to have issue by yours. Besides this, we have been nyne descents Barons and Earls of Stafford, before any Bagot was known in this shire; for Busse, Bagot, and Green were but raised by King Richard II. And to prove that you were no better than vassals to my hows, my Stafford Knot remeyneth still in your parlour, as a hundred of my poor tenants have in sundry shires of England, and have ever held your land of my hows, untill the ateynder of the Duke, my grandfather. Surely I will not exchange my name of Stafford for the name of a 'BAGGE OF OATES,' for that is your name, BAGOTE. Therefore you do me as great wrong in this surmyse as you did with your writing to the Privy-Counsaile to have countenanced that shamefast Higons to charge me with treason, whereof God and my trawthe delyvered me. Your neighbore, I must be.
>
> EDWARD STAFFORD

Bagot, nothing daunted by 'my lord's wrath', but firm in the truth, replied like a well-read genealogist:

> RIGHT HONOURABLE,- I perceave by your letters, delivered to me by your chaplain, Mr. Cope, on Monday last, your Lordship is greatly discontented with some my speeches used to Mr. Stanford, in pretending your honor's surname to be Bagot: I do confess I spake them; and not offending your lordship (as I hope you will not) with trothe I do avowe it. Not upon any 'Dronken Herehaught's report by me corrupted to

soothe my lieing,' but by good records and evidence under ancient seales, the four hundred years past. And if it may please you to send any sufficient man, as Mr. Sheriff, or Mr. Samson Eardswick, Gentillmen of good knowledge and experience in these ac'cons, I will shewe them sufficient matter to confirme that I have spoken; being very sorry to heare your Lordship to contemne and deface the name of Bagot with so bad tirmes and hastie speeches as you do: more dishonourable to yourself than any blemishe or reproche to me: and therefore if your Lordship take it in such disdaine, that I touch you either in credit or honour, you may (if you please) by ordinary process, bring me before the Rt. Hon. the Earl Marshal of England, Chief Judge in these causes, when I will prove it, or take the discredit, with such further punishment as his honour shall inflict upon me.

Thus humbly desireing acceptance of this my answer in good part, till a further triall be had herein, I do comyt your Lordship to the protection of Allmighty, this first of March, 1589.

Your Lordship's at Commandment,
If you please,
RICHARD BAGOT.[15]

When Edward, 4th Lord Stafford, died at Stafford Castle in 1625/6 the heir to the barony was his grandson, a four-year-old boy Henry. As a minor, Henry, together with his sister Mary, became the wards of the Earl Marshal, Thomas Howard 14th Earl of Arundel. This marked the beginning of a new chapter in the history of the Staffords for Henry died aged 16 in 1637, before entering into his inheritance. The Earl of Arundel thereupon arranged a marriage between his own younger son William and Mary Stafford who was the heiress to the remaining Stafford estates. There was a male Stafford heir, Roger, a descendant of the 1st Lord Stafford by one of his younger sons. He was, however, living in obscure circumstances and his sister had married a labourer. Their son was a shoemaker or cobbler. The Stuarts were sensitive concerning the dignity of the peerage and so poor Roger was declared unfit to inherit the title which he was forced to surrender in 1639. Instead it was bestowed by Charles I on Mary, the heiress of the last Lord Stafford, and her new husband William. Roger died in 1641 so his disinheritance was never contested. Mary and William and their heirs were jointly created Baron and Baroness Stafford of new creation and Viscount and Viscountess Stafford in 1640. Mary and her descendants were also the heirs-general to the old Stafford peerage and any of the residual honours of the Buckinghams.[16]

William Howard, the new Lord Stafford, came from a family with an ancestry as grand and tragic as the Buckinghams. He was indeed the great-great-great-grandson of the 3rd Duke of Buckingham through the marriage of that Duke's daughter Lady Elizabeth Stafford to the 3rd (Howard) Duke of Norfolk. John, Lord Howard, the

25 Mary, Countess of
Stafford as a widow.
Portrait by Michael
Wright. (Arundel
Castle)

senior co-heir of the Mowbrays (previous Dukes of Norfolk) and descended through
his mother from Edward I, had been created Duke of Norfolk in 1483 by Richard III
but was killed at the battle of Bosworth. The 2nd Duke had been attainted by
Henry VII but restored after his great victory over the Scots at Flodden in 1513. The
3rd Duke was also attainted for treason but escaped death because Henry VIII died
on the morning his execution was planned, and he was eventually restored by Queen
Mary. He had married the daughter of the last Duke of Buckingham. Their eldest son,
Henry Earl of Surrey, the poet, was, however, executed by Henry VIII for using the
royal arms. The 4th Duke of Norfolk was executed and attainted for plotting to marry
Mary Queen of Scots, in 1572. His son, in turn, Philip, who inherited the Earldom
of Arundel and Arundel Castle in Sussex from his Fitzalan grandfather, was also
condemned of treason (saying prayers for the success of the Spanish Armada) and
died a martyr in the Tower of London never having seen his son Thomas who was
born after his father's imprisonment and brought up in impoverished circumstances
by his pious mother Anne (Dacre) Countess of Arundel. Thomas was restored as 14th
Earl of Arundel by James I and created Earl Marshal, the Great Office of State

26 William, Viscount
Stafford: portrait after
Anthony Van Dyck.
(Arundel Castle)

traditionally vested in the Mowbray and Howard family, just as the Lord High Constable
had been in the Bohuns and Buckinghams.[17]

Lord Arundel outwardly conformed to the Established Church[18] and married a
great catch, Aletheia Talbot, daughter and eventually sole heiress of Gilbert 7th Earl
of Shrewsbury whose northern estates including Sheffield were to more than make
good the losses suffered by the Howards through their 16th-century executions and
attainders. Lord Arundel's driving ambition was to restore the Howard family fully to
its lost greatness and to retrieve the Dukedom of Norfolk. He was eventually to be
successful after his death, when his eldest grandson, 'Little Tom', was restored as 5th
Duke of Norfolk by Charles II at the Restoration in 1660.

The betrothal of Arundel's youngest son William to Mary, the Stafford heiress,
formed part of the plans for the revival and aggrandisement of the Howard family, as
did the creation of William and Mary as Baron and Baroness Stafford by Letters Patent
in 1640 (within a year raised to a Viscounty).[19] So did the assemblage of the great art
collections which were Lord Arundel's passion, and of which the majority were eventually
to be inherited by William and his descendants – not the Dukes of Norfolk.

27 The Earl and Countess of Arundel. They were the parents of Viscount Stafford who inherited from them the celebrated Arundel Collection. By Anthony Van Dyck, 1630. (Arundel Castle)

Lord Arundel was the first of the great English aristocratic collectors and patrons on the Italian model. He assembled the earliest English collection of antique marbles: Greek and Roman statues, busts, architectural fragments, altars and inscribed tablets (many of which are now in the Ashmolean Museum at Oxford). His Old Master Drawings were also outstanding and included the Holbein portrait drawings of Henry VIII's courtiers (now in the Royal Library at Windsor), his paintings included works by most of the Italian and Flemish 16th-century Masters as well as no fewer than 30 portraits by Holbein, while his antique gems were the finest collection ever assembled in England, and his library included *in toto* that of Pirkheimer (the friend and patron of Durer). These books were presented to the Royal Society by his grandson, the 6th Duke of Norfolk, where some of them remain today. Arundel was also the patron of many contemporary artists including the painters Rubens and Van Dyck, the architect Inigo Jones, the sculptor François Dieussart and the engraver Wenceslas Hollar.[20]

Lady Arundel was fond of her younger son William, who seems to have been her favourite and whom she chose as the heir to her personal estate rather than his elder brother Henry Frederick, who succeeded as Earl of Arundel. In her lifetime she showed him many marks of special favour. When he was created a Knight of the Bath in 1629 she gave him a beautifully engraved French astronomical watch which she had commissioned from the famous French clock maker Pierre Combret of Lyons in 1613. She had it engraved with a special inscription: 'From Alethea, Countess of Arundel for her deare son Sir William Howard K B 1629.' This was treasured by Lord Stafford and his descendants and heirs who have inherited it as an heirloom over the centuries. It now belongs to the present Lord Stafford.[21]

Lady Arundel shared her husband's interests in the arts, and was a great patron in her own right, frequently travelling on the Continent independently from her husband, and building her own house in London, Tart Hall, Westminster, adjoining St James's Park on land acquired in 1623 next to what is now Buckingham Palace but which was then a Mulberry Garden. She kept her own collection there, including china

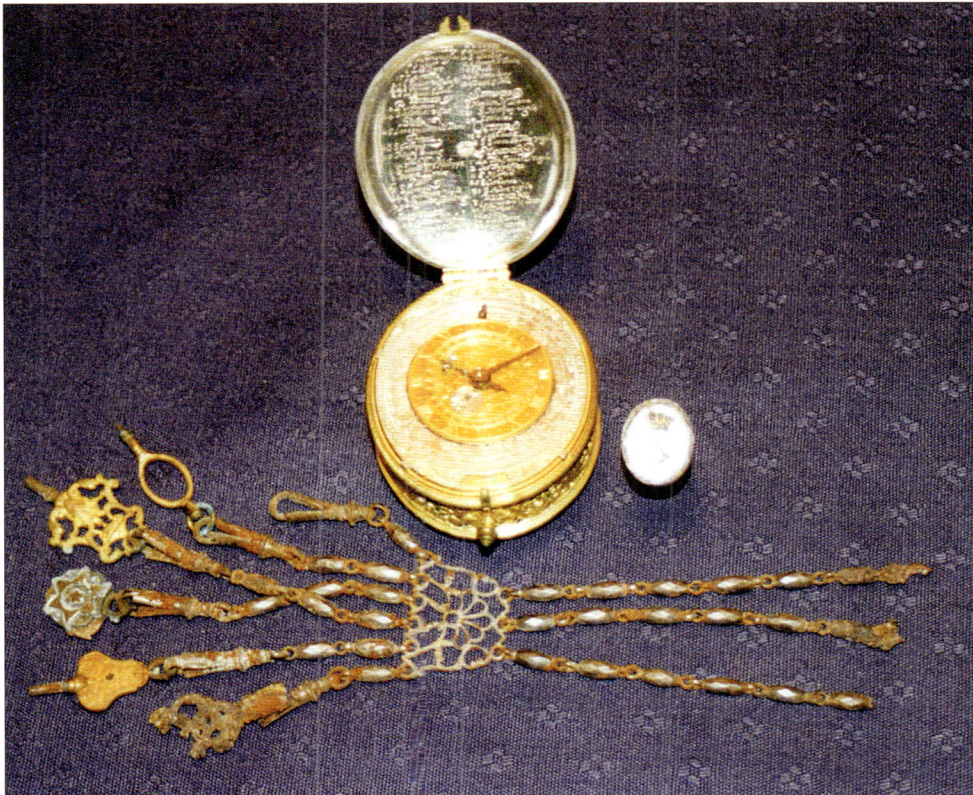

28 French watch given to Viscount Stafford by his mother, the Countess of Arundel, in 1636 when he was made a Knight of the Bath.

29 Founders Kin from the English Dominican Priory at Bornheim, Flanders. Viscount Stafford appears at the bottom left beneath Cardinal Norfolk. (Arundel Castle)

and paintings. In her will she left this house with all her personal estate to her second son William, Viscount Stafford and his wife Mary. Re-named Stafford House, it became the London home of the Stafford Howard family.[22]

Viscount Stafford's and his wife Mary's coming into the Stafford title and Staffordshire estates could not have occurred at a less auspicious moment, coinciding as it did with the outbreak of the English Civil War between Charles I and Parliament. During the early part of the Civil War (1642-3) the castle was held for the Royalist cause by Isobel, Lady Stafford, 'the old lady'. She was the widow of Edward Stafford who had died in 1625. The fortifications were reinforced with earthworks, ditches, timber revetments and stockades for protection against gunfire. Charles I and his nephew, Prince Rupert of the Rhine, visited Stafford in the autumn of 1642 and this, no doubt, provided the impetus for these sophisticated extra defensive works. The royalist garrison, nevertheless, were unable to maintain their position and the castle was taken by the Parliamentarians in 1643 and subsequently 'slighted' or dismantled.[23] On 23 December 1643 the castle was ordered to be demolished so that it would not again be used as a stronghold. It was largely destroyed and the materials were taken away, leaving only the foundations and lowest parts of the walls up to the ground-floor level, with the outline of the rectangular hall block and five towers. This act of vandalism more-or-less ruined one of the most perfect small 14th-century secular buildings in England.

Both Mary and William were staunchly Catholic. Lord Arundel's family had not followed his outward conformity to the Church of England. One reason why Lady Arundel built her own house in London, away from Arundel House in the Strand, was so that she could receive priests there and meet other Catholics without embarrassing her husband, the Earl Marshal, whose rivals at Court would have made capital out of any suggestion that he was a 'papist'. The penal laws worked less harshly against married women, as their legal status was less clearly defined and they were usually given the benefit of the doubt and assumed to be of the same persuasion as their husbands.[24] As royalists and Catholics, the Staffords were doubly likely to be 'sequestered persons', and following the example of the elderly Lord and Lady Arundel they left England and went into exile on the continent at the beginning of the Civil War.

In Viscount Stafford's own words:

> In the beginning of the late unhappy times thinking my prescence might prejudice rather than serve the King, my wife and I settled at Antwerp when the war began, where we might have lived obscurely but safely. My conscience was not satisfied to see my King in such disorder, and I not endeavour to serve him what I could to free him from his troubles. And I did come into England and served His Majesty faithfully and loyally as long as he lived.[25]

He saw service in the royal army, and at Naseby was in charge of the young princes.

In July 1647 he returned to Flanders to collect his wife and children. There were eight Stafford Howard children in all: Henry, John Francis, Aletheia, Isabella, Ursula, Anastasia, Helena, and Mary. They were educated by the Augustinian Canonesses at St Monica, Louvain, where the mother superior Magdalen Throckmorton was a cousin of Lady Stafford. Several of the girls later became nuns, Aletheia joining the Augustinian Canonesses in Paris and Mary, the youngest, a Dominican at Spellikens founded by her cousin Cardinal Philip Howard (younger brother of the 5th Duke of Norfolk). The Cardinal restored the English Dominican province with two houses in Flanders, one for men, one for nuns. This continental education, and the admission of younger children to English religious houses in Flanders and Paris was to be a continuous feature of the family history of the Stafford Howards and the Jerninghams,

30 Map of the Shifnal Estate in Shropshire bequeathed to Viscount Stafford by his mother, the Countess of Arundel, and which has descended with the Stafford title ever since. (Arundel Castle)

who succeeded them, down to the end of the 18th century and the French Revolution. The combination of a cosmopolitan outlook and continental ramifications, together with their more strictly circumscribed life as Catholic recusants in England makes this later family history so unusual and so fascinating. The Stafford Howards and their heirs, the Jerninghams, married into the French aristocracy and had continental military and ecclesiastical connections. They were both much more closely involved in the mainstream of continental Catholicism therefore than most English 'recusants' who often lived very narrow provincial lives in England in the 17th and 18th centuries, excluded by their religion from involvement in public or political life and prevented from serving in the British army. The Stafford family partly made up for this, by serving the French and Austrian monarchies and by part living on the continent.

After the execution of the King, and during the Commonwealth, Viscount and Viscountess Stafford remained on the continent, travelling around from country to country: Flanders, France, Italy, Germany. In 1649 they were in Rome where Lord Stafford was present at the patronal Feast of St Thomas of Canterbury at the English College. The following summer they stayed in his father's old villa at Padua, where Lord Arundel had died in 1646 and where his affairs were still being sorted. Lady Stafford then returned to London with the children, but her husband continued on the continent where he was employed on diplomatic business by the Holy Roman Emperor's Court. In 1652 he was at Heidelberg, 'a narrow Calvinist' place, where he was imprisoned for 13 months but never brought to trial. On his release (at a cost of £1,000 put up by his mother) in 1653 he went straight to Frankfurt to report to the Emperor, and from there back to Holland. He was with his mother Aletheia in Holland when she died on 3 June 1654. She made him her sole legatee, to pay her

31 The Earl of Arundel and his family. Viscount Stafford holds the 16th-century Pagant shield which became one of the great treasures of the Stafford Collection. Painted by Fruytiers. (Arundel Castle)

debts and do all he 'knew or believed to be her desire'. Lady Arundel's will was the cause of a series of lawsuits between Viscount Stafford and other members of the Howard family.[26]

Viscount Stafford's elder brother, Henry Frederick, Earl of Arundel had already contested the old Earl's will, which had left the collection and a life interest in the estates to Aletheia. Three years of litigation had followed, and Henry Frederick had lost. Following his death in 1652 the worries and untied ends were inherited by Henry Frederick's second son Lord Henry, an energetic 24-year-old who managed the family affairs and was eventually to succeed his incapacitated brother as 6th Duke of Norfolk. Lord Stafford's involvement in the aftermath of this litigation embittered relations with his nephews. He took his mother's side, because – as he said – she 'had brought great estates to her husband and the bequest to her was therefore fair'. This contrary standpoint was exacerbated by his lack of tact and ill temper. As Evelyn remarked later: 'Lord Stafford was not a man beloved, especially by his own family.' The reasons for this and his tragic end are best traced in a separate chapter.

VI

*Viscount Stafford
and the Earls of Stafford*

⮿ · ⮾

W HEN WILLIAM, Viscount Stafford finally returned to England after the
Civil War and Commonwealth, a period of nearly twenty years' warfare, exile,
imprisonment, foreign travel and lawsuits, he was an embittered and disappointed
man. His marriage in 1637 and the Stafford title had promised so much, but had
brought him nothing but hardship. Stafford Castle had been razed to the ground by
the Cromwellians. His bequest from his mother of the lion's share of the Arundel
Collection and her splendid house in Westminster had also turned out to be a bugbear,
poisoned by legal disputes, family ill-feeling and a multitude of buzzing creditors. His
father, the old Earl of Arundel, who had died in exile in Padua in 1646, had left debts
of £200,000 so that the poor aged Countess in her last days in the Low Countries had
been unable to secure any of the money due to her under her husband's will and had
been forced to live by selling or pawning items from the collection. When the
Arundels left England in 1641 they had taken with them the lion's share of the
collection : nearly 400 paintings, 1,200 prints and drawings, gold and silver plate, and
the antique gems, all valued at over £100,000.[1] Only the library and the statues had
been left behind at Arundel House to fare as best they could.

In 1655 the bailiffs arrived at Tart Hall to satisfy the family's creditors. Though
sequestered by Parliament, Tart Hall was leased to Mary Viscountess Stafford on her
return to London in 1650. In Holland, where Lady Arundel had houses at Amersfort
and Amsterdam, her late husband's scholarly librarian, Francis Junius, was claiming the
arrears of his salary for 23 years' service and the return of the manuscript of his
masterwork on the Saxon languages which he had prepared under the Arundels'
patronage. Junius complained of 'the barbarous and most wretched unthankfulness of
the Viscount Stafford, who brags of having the manuscript and jokes about it' and the
'unhandsome dealings of the late juggling countess and her wretchedly ungrateful son'.
Lord Stafford's nephews, Henry (later 6th Duke of Norfolk and the manager of the

family affairs as Tom, the oldest son, was mentally unstable following an illness contracted while studying at Padua University) and Charles had claimed half the personal estate in Holland. This sparked off a series of further lawsuits, some of which Stafford won and some were left unresolved until the English Court of Delegates eventually acknowledged his right to administer his mother's estates and to recover the arrears due to her under Lord Arundel's will. In compensation Viscount Stafford allowed Henry to have the cabinet of gems, and Charles, the fourth son of Henry Frederick, two portraits and an agate cup.[2]

The problem was made worse by the fact that under the Commonwealth the Stafford Howard estates in England had all been sequestered, so there was no landed income, and the teeming creditors could only be paid by selling or pawning things. In 1656 Lord Stafford was imprisoned in Utrecht for debt. All this exacerbated his tendency to ill temper. He quarrelled furiously with his nephew Henry and fell out with the English Jesuits for not sending a witness to England to support him in his law suit, despite the fact that for a Jesuit to visit England during the Commonwealth would have meant risking his life. He never spoke to the Jesuits again during the remaining 25 years of his life.

Eventually, however, the family affairs were sorted out and Viscount Stafford inherited Tart Hall and the Arundel Collection, as well as some of his mother's lands including the manor of Shifnall in Shropshire, and a third of the manor of Wrockwardine. The former was a Dacre property which had belonged to Anne (Dacre) Countess of Arundel, the Collector's mother, and which she had bequeathed to Aletheia, and the latter was a Talbot property inherited from Gilbert 7th Earl of Shrewsbury.[3] Lord Stafford inherited both these properties from his mother. The Shifnall estate has descended with the Stafford title ever since: to the Jerninghams in the 18th century, then to the Fitzherberts in the twentieth. His mother's bequest to William made him a rich man, for her personal estate had been estimated at £60,000 in May 1654.[4]

Viscount Stafford was, naturally, a strong supporter of Charles II and the Restoration of the monarchy. In February 1659/60, in a confidential report to the King, he was described as being 'wholly devoted to Your Majesty's Service as far as his power and interest can enable him'. He took part in the royal procession when Charles II returned to London in triumph on 29 May 1660.

On 5 June 1660 the Staffords' lands were all restored to them, but William was not satisfied with this. He pushed his wife's claim to an earldom, but this was disallowed in 1664. He harboured resentment at this seeming royal ingratitude. Bishop Burnet noted that Stafford 'thought the King had not rewarded him for his former services as they deserved. So he often voted against the King, and made great applications always to the Earl of Shaftesbury.'[5] Thus he added political opposition and disaffection to the other feuds and grudges with his family, his father's former employees, religious orders like the Jesuits and everybody else whom he thought had crossed or ill-treated him.

32 Philip Howard, Cardinal Norfolk. Viscount Stafford travelled to Rome for his nephew's installation as a cardinal. (Arundel Castle)

Though to outsiders like Evelyn or Burnet, Stafford seemed an irascible, harsh and cantankerous man, these aspects of his character were balanced by a softer side, which was shown in his touching affection for his wife and children. He was a loving husband and a doting father. The arranged marriage to Mary Stafford could have been a cold formality but developed into an undoubted love match. In his last letter to her, while awaiting death in the Tower of London, he wrote: 'Were I to live numbers of years, I would never omit to let you know the love I bear to you.' He was a generous and devoted father who frequently travelled to see his children at school on the continent. He and several of the family were present when his daughter Lady Ursula Stafford Howard was clothed as an Augustinian nun at St Monica's, Louvain on 4 September 1663. He was happy in the company of his wife and children. The tribulations during enforced exile and the troubles over the Arundel wills, while hardening Lord Stafford's outer shell, cemented the bonds with his own immediate family.

Nor did he fall out with all his nephews. He was a firm supporter of Philip, the youngest of the Collector Earl of Arundel's grandsons who became a priest and a Dominican. When Philip was made a Cardinal in 1675 Stafford and his youngest son John went openly to Rome to support him and were present for the ceremony when Philip received the Red Hat from the Pope. Cardinal Norfolk, as he was called, played a significant behind-the-scenes role in late 17th-century Anglo-Roman relations, among other things organising the marriage of James II to Mary of Modena. The visits of

English relations like Viscount Stafford were therefore a useful means of communi-cation between Rome and London.[6]

His short temper and irascibility were rooted in ill health. He was plagued by strange allergies and suffered from 'gout' for which he took the waters in Bath. John Evelyn, the diarist and a protegé of old Lord Arundel's, describes an extraordinary occasion in 1670 when Viscount Stafford was dining at Goring House (next door to Tart Hall) with the Earl of Arlington, Charles II's minister. 'Lord Stafford arose from the table in some disorder, because roses were stuck about the fruit when the dessert came upon the table.' He was allergic to roses.

Viscount Stafford was an unlikely candidate for heroic martyrdom, but he was to be the last of the Howards and the Staffords to be executed. He met his end on trumped up charges of treason and was condemned to death by his peers under the familiar machinery of judicial murder which the Tudors had perfected. He was to be caught up in the machinations of the Titus Oates plot and chosen, as the Catholic peer least likely to put up a good legal defence, for a show treason trial in Westminster Hall.

The Test Act of 1678 excluded Catholics from both Houses of Parliament, and effectively debarred English Catholics from any role in public affairs for the next hundred years. This was a response to increased anti-Catholic feeling in the country; this hysteria was successfully exploited by Titus Oates, a lapsed Catholic and perjurer. He accused the English Catholics of a plot to murder the King, the Archbishop of Canterbury and all the leading Protestant statesmen and divines. Oates repeated these allegations before a magistrate on oath on 6 September 1678 and to the Privy Council on 25 October that year. On the strength of his unfounded and incredible accusations, Viscount Stafford and four other Catholic peers[7] were arrested and imprisoned in the King's Bench, from where Stafford was taken to the Tower of London pending trial for treason. He spent a year and a half in the Tower of London with some detriment to his health and eyesight though, apart from the curtailment of his freedom, conditions there were not harsh. He could have escaped to the continent but felt so strong a sense of his own innocence that he did not attempt to flee. In the autumn of 1678 when Oates claimed that Stafford was plotting the assassination of the King, he had taken the waters in Bath for his gout, visited his Anglican kinsman the 1st Duke of Beaufort at Badminton, and stayed with the Catholic Lord Aston at Tixall near Stafford. Lord Aston's steward, Stephen Dugdale claimed that at Tixall Nicholas Furnese (Lord Stafford's Dutch secretary) had approached him with secret treasonous proposals, and that Viscount Stafford intended to kill the King. Dugdale 'plunged himself into deep and horrid oaths, not only untrue, but morally impossible to be true'. On the strength of these flimsy allegations Viscount Stafford was brought to trial in Westminster Hall on 30 November 1680, the feast of St Andrew. He was then 68 years old. Much is known about the trial and the last weeks of Viscount Stafford's life, from a number of contemporary memoirs and pamphlets, including one written by his Benedictine confessor, Dom Maurus Corker.[8] There is also the official account in the printed *State Trials*, and eye-witness reports such as John Evelyn's diaries. Two of Stafford's own daughters attended the trial and made notes: the Marchioness of Winchester and Lady Anastasia Stafford Howard.

Viscount Stafford was 'no great rhetorician nor much versed in the law'. The peers (his judges), were cowed by anti-popery riots outside and popular ill-feeling against Catholics. Stafford found himself pitted against a posse of skilled and experienced lawyers, but was not himself allowed to cross question the witnesses to reveal the inconsistency and general contradictions of their implausible assertions. The trial itself lasted for five days. On the fourth day Stafford summed up his defence. Evelyn noted that 'he spoke a great while, but confusedly and without any method ... One thing he said, as to Oates, did exceedingly affect me – that such a hypocrite that had so deeply prevaricated as even to turn idolater (for so we of the Church of England term it) and protest before God so solemnly that he was entirely theirs – I say the fitness of such a wretch should not be admitted against the life of a peer, this must need's redound to the dishonour of our religion and verily I am of his Lordship's opinion that such a man's testimony should not be taken against the life of a dog.'[9]

Judgement was declared on the fifth day by the Lord Chancellor who had presided as High Steward. Though many impartial observers had been struck by the inconsistencies and obvious untruths in the evidence of the three witnesses – Titus Oates, Stephen Dugdale and Edward Turberville – Stafford was nevertheless found guilty by 55 to 31 votes. He responded to the Lord Chancellor's pronouncement: 'My Lord, I have very little to say; I confess I am surprised at it for I did not expect it. But God's will be done, and your Lordships; I will not murmur at it. God forgive those who have sworn against me.' The King, unlike his subjects, believed in Stafford's innocence but could do no more than commute the sentence from hanging, drawing and quartering to simple beheading.

The execution of Viscount Stafford took place on Tower Hill on Wednesday 29 December 1680 and is as well recorded as his trial had been by his contemporaries. In the time left to him in the Tower, Stafford prepared himself for death by prayer and recollection, and put his affairs in order, writing to his wife and children and drafting his last speech for the scaffold.[10] According to Fr Corker, he saw his forthcoming execution as an atonement for his past sins and himself as a martyr for his Catholic beliefs: 'I conceive this Sentence is fallen upon me upon account of the Religion I am of; if I had numbers of lives, I would lose them all, rather than forsake that Church, that I am of; and which I am well assured that it maintains nothing but what is warranted by the Word of God.'[11] He was to be beatified in the 20th century by the Pope as one of the English Reformation martyrs.

His imprisonment in the Tower, like that of many state prisoners, was relatively comfortable. Cosimo III, Grand Duke of Tuscany, continued to send him the customary consignment of 'most excellent wine' while he was in gaol, awaiting execution.[12] He supped well and slept well the night before his death, according to Bishop Burnet's

The Tryall of William Howard L:ᵈ Viscount Stafford in Westminster hall. 1680

His Execution on Tower hill.

high Steward.
The Peers in ᵧ Robes.
CC The Commons.
D The Judges.
E The Prisoner.
F The K:ˢ Box.
G The Managers of ᵧ Impeach
H The Evidence.

33 The trial and execution of Viscount Stafford in 1680. (Arundel Castle)

34 Isabella, Marchioness of Winchester and daughter of Viscount Stafford, who attended his trial in Westminster Hall, writing an eye-witness account. Portrait by John Hayls.

35 Sixteenth-century gold and enamel IHS badge worn by Viscount Stafford at his execution. This sacred relic in the family was made for Anne, Countess of Arundel, the patron of the English Jesuits. She bequeathed it to her daughter-in-law Aletheia who in turn left it to Viscount Stafford. (By kind permission of Victoria & Albert Museum; photograph: Diana Scarisbrick)

memoirs, and showed no signs of fear, but to the last behaved calmly and composedly, fortified by the sense of his own innocence; something which was remarked on by all onlookers. The 29th December was a cold day. At 10 o'clock he was collected by the Lieutenant of the Tower and conveyed to the two sheriffs with whom he processed through lines of horse and foot guards to the scaffold. A large mob surrounded the place of execution. To the crowds he appeared extremely unconcerned. 'He looked Death in the face with so undaunted a resolution … Grace had left him no resentments of Nature.'

He was smartly dressed in a cablet coat, silk embroidered waistcoat, a brown periwig hat, and a diamond IHS jewel on his breast. On the scaffold he read his speech and reiterated his innocence: 'I am as Innocent as it is possible for any man to be … of the Crimes laid to my charge … I have a great confidence that it will please Almighty God in a short time to bring truth to light. Then all the world will see and know what injury has been done me.'[13] He then knelt and said his prayers in Latin and made the sign of the cross. The executioner severed the head with a single blow but some of the skin at the throat not being chopped through he cut it with a knife before holding up the head at the four corners of the scaffold: 'Here is the Head of a Traytor, here is the Head of a Traytor against the King.' The body was left for 15 minutes for the blood to drain, and then placed in an elm coffin with the initials 'W.S. 1680' on the lid.

36 Lady Aletheia Stafford, daughter of Viscount Stafford. She became an Augustinian canoness in Paris, one of several Stafford Howard nuns. Portrait by Jacob Hysman.

37 The Hon. John Stafford-Howard, second son of Viscount Stafford, 1664. Portrait by Isaac Fuller.

38 The Hon. Francis Stafford-Howard, the third son of Viscount Stafford, and Groom of the Bed Chamber to King James II. Portrait by Henri Gascar.

39 Henry, 1st Earl of Stafford. He was created Earl of Stafford in 1688 and accompanied James II into exile at Saint Germain. Portrait by Thomas Pooley.

The shirt, rings, watch and I.H.S. jewel worn by Viscount Stafford on the scaffold were bequeathed to his family and were long-treasured as relics and heirlooms among his descendants. At the English Dominican convent at Spellikens, near Brussels, his younger daughter Sister Delphine herself read aloud to the nuns in the refectory the news of her father's execution, 'without a break in her voice. And the anguish of the effort turned her hair snow-white.' She was 22 years old.

No one knows where the martyred Viscount Stafford was buried. His grave is not in the Tower of London. Mary Stafford kept the secret of the whereabouts of her husband's coffin. It is thought that it may be in St Edward's Chapel at Westminster Abbey, close to the tomb of the Stafford's royal ancestor, Eleanor Duchess of Gloucester; for there Lady Stafford herself was to be buried in 1693, her son Henry in 1719 and grandson John in 1762.

James II, after his accession to the throne, as a sort of belated apology for her husband's unjust execution, created Mary Countess of Stafford in her own right. In October 1688 her eldest son Henry was created an Earl with succession to his heirs male. A bill was also passed in the House of Lords to reverse the attainder against Viscount Stafford but not carried into effect because of the political upheavals of the

40 Lady Mary Stafford Howard, daughter of the
1st Earl of Stafford who married Guy, Count de
Rohan Chabot.

41 Ann, Countess of Stafford as a shepherdess,
wife of the 2nd Earl. They lived mainly in France
and sold the collection at Stafford House. Portrait
by Johannes Verelst.

time. The historical result of this anomaly was that, though Mary was a Countess in
her own right and her male descendants were to be Earls of Stafford, the barony itself
remained under attainder for the best part of one and a half centuries.

Henry, 1st Earl of Stafford (1647-1719) was among the small group of English
Catholics, including Lady Strickland of Sizergh and the Earl of Powis, who accompanied
James II into exile at Saint Germain. He was with the deposed Stuart king at his death
bed and was a witness to his will. A romantic devotion to the legitimacy of the Stuart
cause was to be nurtured by future generations, alongside their recusant Catholicism,
as an aspect of their loyalty to ancestral truths and rights which resulted in exclusion
from English public affairs and bouts of self-imposed exile. Henry himself died in
1719 and was buried alongside his mother (and possibly his father) in Westminster
Abbey. He married a French noblewoman, Claude Charlotte, eldest daughter of Philibert
Comte de Grammont, but they had no children, so he was succeeded by his nephew
William as 2nd Earl of Stafford. The 2nd Earl in turn married his cousin Ann, daughter
of George Holman and Anastasia Stafford Howard. William 2nd Earl of Stafford was

42 John Paul, 4th and Last Earl of Stafford. On his death in 1762 the Earldom became extinct. Portrait by William Hoare.

43 Elizabeth, Countess of Stafford, wife of the 4th Earl. Portrait by William Hoare, 1758.

the son of John Stafford Howard (younger son of the 1st Earl) who had died in Paris in 1714 and is buried in the church of St Sulpice. His predominant residence in France, and the family's coming and going between England and the continent, established an unusual pattern which lasted through much of the 18th century. John Stafford Howard's younger daughters Louisa and Xaveria both became nuns in Paris, members of the Order of the Immaculate Conception or 'Blue Nuns', an order founded in 1658 and so called from the colour of their habits. The 2nd and 3rd Earls of Stafford and their families lived mainly in France, and several daughters married into the French aristocracy or entered French convents. They were in many ways more French than English.

The 2nd Earl is best remembered, however, not for his French domicile or religious affiliations, but for his sale in 1720 of the Arundel Collection inherited from Countess Aletheia and preserved at Stafford House, London (formerly Tart Hall). A copy of the sale catalogue, enumerating large quantities of paintings, engravings, drawings, bronzes, medals, porcelain and curiosities, is preserved in the British Library, and the dispersal took several days to complete.[14] The house itself was demolished and the site sold in 1742-3 as recorded by the antiquary George Vertue who made notes on the demolition.[15] This marked the sad end of the first and greatest of the English aristocratic art collections, an assemblage which had until then survived Civil War, near-bankruptcy, foreign exile and prolonged law-suits, but which now succumbed

44 Mary (Plowden), Lady Jerningham, niece of the last Earl of Stafford, through whom the claim to the Stafford barony was inherited by the Jerninghams.

to the 2nd Earl's shortage of money and lack of interest. He continued to sell family property throughout his life, including Thornbury Castle in Gloucestershire to his cousin the 8th Duke of Norfolk in 1727, and the great Van Dyck portrait of the Collector Earl of Arundel and 'Little Tom', and the Italian 16th-century pageant shield to the 9th Duke of Norfolk (who was his principal trustee). Several of the most important Howard family heirlooms now at Arundel Castle were acquired in these years by the Dukes of Norfolk from their impoverished Stafford cousins who had inherited them from the Collector Earl's younger son, William Viscount Stafford.[16]

The 2nd Earl died in 1734 and bequeathed his remaining English property, including the manor of Shifnall in Shropshire and the ruins of Stafford Castle, and heirloom plate, books and chattels, to his eldest son William Matthias, who became 3rd Earl of Stafford.[17] He died in 1750 without legitimate male issue, though he had an illegitimate son William, born in 1742. The 3rd Earl was buried in the ancestral vault of the Fitzalans and the Howards at Arundel in Sussex. As he had no legitimate son he was succeeded as 4th and last Earl of Stafford by his uncle John Paul, the second son of John Stafford Howard who had died in Paris in 1724. He, too, had no sons but three daughters and on his death in 1762 the earldom became extinct. Of his daughters, the eldest, Mary Apollonia, married the French nobleman Rohan de Chabot, but they had no children and she died in 1769. The two younger – Anne and Anastasia – became Blue Nuns in Paris like their aunts. His younger sister Mary, however, married Francis Plowden of Plowden in Shropshire whose daughter, also Mary, married Sir George Jerningham of Costessey in Norfolk. As a result of this, the Jerninghams became heirs general to the attainted barony of Stafford, and inherited the Shifnall and Stafford Castle estates in 1769.

VII

The Jerninghams

❧ · ❧

WITH THE GEORGIAN JERNINGHAMS – 'the branch on which the long-attainted title blossomed once more' – we are confronted for the first time in the Stafford history with fully rounded human beings whose loves, sorrows and happinesses, ambitions and sense of humour seem sympathetic to a modern reader. Their portraits, journals, and many letters survive and give a more complete picture than of any of their medieval, Tudor or Stuart ancestors. Like their predecessors they too had maintained faithfully a Catholic recusant tradition.

In 1719 the 2nd Earl of Stafford wrote to his son, William Mathias: 'My dearest son, as it has been God's Mercy to keep your ancestors and family in the holy religion, fear the heaviest judgement upon the man who forsakes it for vile unchristian motives … Adhere to it by profession and practice, and serve God in the old, only true way.'[1] This was an injunction that most of his descendants took to heart.

The Jerninghams were a Norfolk knightly family who had remained Catholic after the 16th-century reformation and split of the English church. Like the Staffords and Howards, they too could trace their ancestry back to the early Middle Ages.[2] Their first recorded ancestor was Hubert Gernegan (the original spelling of the name), who held a knight's fee of the Suffolk Honour of Eye in 1183. The founder of the Costessey branch of the family was Sir Henry Jerningham (died 1571), eldest son of Sir Edward Jernegan of Somerleyton and Huntingfield, Suffolk, by his second wife Mary, daughter of Lord Scrope of Bolton (Yorkshire). Sir Henry was one of the first to declare for Queen Mary on the death of Edward VI and raised East Anglia in her support. She was then resident at Kenninghall, near the Norfolk-Suffolk border. Sir Henry went to her and offered his services, and was appointed captain of her guard. He accompanied the Queen from Yarmouth to London for her coronation, and defended her from various attempted rebellions. He defeated Wyatt at Charing Cross in 1554.

For his loyalty and good service he was knighted, appointed to the Privy Council and made Vice Chamberlain and Master of the Royal Household, and granted several manors in Suffolk and Norfolk including Cossey or Costessey in 1555. He rebuilt Costessey Hall in 1564 as an H-plan red-brick house in the Tudor style, and this mid-16th-century house remained the seat of the family, little altered into the 18th century. The Jerninghams were created baronets by James I in 1621, but their religion subsequently

45 Costessey Hall, Norfolk: the old 17th-century Catholic chapel in the attic.

46 Costessey Hall, Norfolk, with the new Catholic chapel designed by Edward Jerningham on the left.

47 Tower in Costessey Park designed by Sir William Jerningham. Painted by J.C. Buckler.

disbarred them from public life in England, from royal service in the Army, and restricted their marriages in the 17th and early 18th centuries to other prominent Catholic recusant families, including the Throckmortons, Blounts and Bedingfelds. They were thus to an extent typical of the 17th- and 18th-century English Catholic gentry who lived quietly on their estates, after a continental education. Strait finances prevented them from modernising their house in the early 18th century. In the second half of the century, however, their inheritance of the Stafford Howard estates (in 1769), and then the gradual relaxation of the penal laws against Catholics from the 1770s onwards (the First Catholic Relief Act was in 1778), marked the beginning of an age of renewed prosperity for the Jerninghams which culminated in the successful resuscitation of the Stafford barony for them at the beginning of the 19th century.

After the death of the 4th Earl of Stafford and the extinction of the earldom, the barony (which was not restricted by a male entail), but for the 1680 attainder against Viscount Stafford, would have been inherited by Lady Anastasia Stafford Howard (daughter of William, 4th and last Earl who had died in 1762) but she was a nun in Paris and took no steps to claim or revive the title. She lived to the good age of 85, surviving the French Revolution (during which upheaval she had remained in France). She eventually died in Paris in 1807. The Jerninghams, however, were her acknowledged

48 Queen Mary Tudor, who gave Costessey to the Jerninghams.

heirs. The last Earl's younger sister Mary, it will be recalled, had married Francis Plowden of Plowden. The Plowden's only son, Francis, became a Catholic priest in France and their eldest daughter, Louisa, did not marry, leaving just the younger daughter Mary, who married Sir George Jerningham 5th Baronet in 1733. Under the 1640 patent of creation the barony could pass to heirs general (male and female), not only to heirs male, and thus could be inherited through the female line.

Sir George and Mary had an eldest son, William Jerningham, born in 1736, who succeeded his father as 6th Baronet in 1774. He and his generation of the Jerninghams, heirs in waiting to the Stafford barony, were remarkably interesting and sympathetic. One of Sir William's brothers, Charles, was a general in the French army and a Knight of Malta. He was Maréchal de Camp and commanded the regiments of Buckley and Navarre. The family nicknamed him 'the Chevalier'. The other brother, Edward, was nicknamed 'the Poet'. He was a writer and a fashionable man of letters in London with a string of plays and theological treatises as well as verses to his name. He was a friend of Horace Walpole's and Lord Chesterfield's. Sir William and 'the Chevalier' were Catholic but 'the Poet' conformed to Anglicanism at the time of George III's coronation in 1761, impressed – it is said – by the splendour of the ceremony at Westminster Abbey. Both Sir William and the Chevalier were professed Knights of Malta, Sir

49 Family group of Sir George Jerningham, his wife Mary (Plowden) and sons, Sir William, Edward ('the poet') and Charles ('the Chevalier'). Painted by John Theodore Hearns.

William having joined the Order in 1751. This, too, was unusual among English Catholics, there being barely half a dozen English members of the Order between the 17th and early 19th centuries and all those had strong continental connections.

Sir William himself had served in the Chevaux-Légers de la Maison de Louis XV, so was a retired cavalry officer. His portraits show him to have been remarkably handsome, another Jerningham trait. He married the Hon Frances Dillon, daughter of the 11th Viscount Dillon, of an Irish family which had lived in France since being driven out of their native land, County Mayo, by Cromwell in the 17th century. They too had strong military traditions. They were the proprietors and hereditary colonels of their own private army, 'Dillon's Regiment', in the service of the kings of France. Frances became the matriarch of English Catholic Society and was nicknamed by the family 'Her Most Catholic Majesty' in a joky allusion to the Kings of France and Spain. Her relations, perhaps even more than the Jerninghams, encompassed a remarkable range of interesting people, more Europeans than English as many of them were resident on the continent in the service of the French and Austrian monarchies; though her eldest brother, the 12th Viscount Dillon, having inherited the Ditchley estate in Oxfordshire through their mother, the Lee heiress, conformed to the Anglican church. Lady Jerningham's father and several of her uncles and brothers, however, were all Colonels in succession to Dillon's Regiment in the service of Louis XV and Louis XVI. Her brother James Dillon was killed at the Battle of Fontenoy. Her younger brother, Arthur, was 6th (and last) Colonel from the age of 17 and also became Governor of St Christopher and Tobago, which were then French colonies. Her uncle, the Abbé Dillon, was a most distinguished French prelate who became Archbishop and Duke of Narbonne and Primate of the Gauls, Commander of the Order of the St Esprit (the French equivalent of the Garter) and President of the States of Languedoc. He was the last Primate of France before the French Revolution and, somewhat unexpectedly, is buried in St Pancras churchyard in London. *The Gentleman's Magazine* announced his death on 5 July 1806: 'At his house in George Street Portman Square Arthur Richard Dillon, Archbishop and Duke of Narbonne, Primate of the Gauls, President of the States of Languedoc, and Commander of the Order of the Holy Ghost.' Such rolling *ancien régime* titles seemed especially incongruous in a circumscribed bricky London setting. A pontifical requiem mass was celebrated at the French Chapel in George Street (one of the public Catholic embassy chapels allowed in London under the terms of the Treaty of Utrecht 1713). He was described as an eloquent preacher and man of letters, of a 'pleasing temper'.[3]

Much is known about this generation of the Jerningham family and their cousins, as large quantities of their correspondence, especially that of Frances Lady Jerningham, survive and were published in the late 19th century. Their letters capture much of their character: their intelligence, unaffected charm, simplicity of manner, kindness, devout religious opinions, and affectionate natures. Cosmopolitan and well-educated, the Georgian Jerninghams had nothing of the narrow or provincial outlook of some English Catholic squirarchical families. They were *au fait* with all the latest news on the continent and at home, from events in France, or later of Napoleon's campaigns, the election of Pope Pius VII in 1800, news of the Austrian court and camp from Vienna or the English court and politics to the latest scientific and medical discoveries. 'The Cow Pox appears to be in universal Practice and I believe that Doctor Jenner is going to have a premium from Parliament for having Discovered so useful a muzzle for the dreadful disorder.'[4]

Sir William and his brothers were educated at the English College at Douai (the forerunner of Stonyhurst) and in Paris. His children, too, were educated in France. They had all thus been exposed to the stimulus of the French Enlightenment: French literature, natural science and European history, rather than the narrow diet of classics which formed the bedrock of English education at the time. It is a generally unremarked fact that later 18th-century English Catholic landowners, such as the Jerninghams and their circle, were often better educated and more widely-read than their average Anglican neighbours. Men like Charles Townley, Henry Blundell or the 11th Duke of Norfolk corresponded with French intellectuals and collected French books.

The Stafford Jerninghams of the late 18th and early 19th centuries moved easily in English society, mixing with their Anglican neighbours at all levels from Court to

50 Edward Jerningham, 'The Poet', 1763. He became an Anglican after witnessing the coronation of George III.

51 Charles Jerningham, 'The Chevalier', 1763, wearing the insignia of a Knight of Malta. He fought in the French army.

village. They were friends of the Royal Family, their Norfolk neighbours including the Anglican Bishop of Norwich, and maintained easy relations with their tenants. In 1803 Lady Jerningham in a letter to her daughter Charlotte described a typical Costessey occasion: 'Your father gave a Barrel of Beer in your Ball Room to the village and danced himself till near 10.'[5] They were without prejudices. On another occasion Lady Jerningham described the Fergussans, plantation owners from the West Indies, turning up to Mass 'with a Black footman who is quite a saint'.[6]

The parents of Sir William, Sir George 5th Bt and Mary (Plowden), had lived at Cambrai in northern France in the 1740s. William and his brothers Charles and Edward therefore grew up proficient in French and Italian, as well as Greek and Latin. The 'Chevalier' and Sir William's uncle, an officer in the imperial army in Vienna, used French as their first language and always corresponded in that tongue. After the death of Sir George (William's father) in January 1774, Mary Lady Jerningham set up house in Grosvenor Square, London, with her youngest son Edward, 'the Poet,' who never married. He lived with her till her death in 1785 when he moved to a house of his own in Green Street, round the corner. This was a typical bachelor residence and was later described by his niece, Charlotte Bedingfeld, as 'dirty but well filled with books and contains some interesting pictures and drawings'.[7]

Edward, 'The Poet' (1727-1812), had an endearingly quirky character with independent views verging on the eccentric, such as the adoption of Anglicanism in the face of his family's feelings. He spent his time writing verse, practising on the harp, frequenting the theatre and opera and corresponding with or visiting family and friends. His circle included the Earl of Chesterfield, the Earl of Carlisle, Earl Harcourt, the Countesses of Ailesbury, Mount Edgcumbe and Jersey. He was also on intimate terms with the Prince of Wales, later George IV, and catalogued the library at Brighton Pavilion for him. His diary survives in a private collection.[8]

His poetry has not stood the test of time and much of it was competent pastiche or even plagiarism. His early work, such as 'The Magdalens' and 'The Nunnery', were close imitations of Gray's *Elegy*, full of fashionable Georgian sentiment; a contemporary critic described him as 'weeping o'er lovelorn oxen and deserted sheep'.[9] His plays included a number of historical tragedies such as 'Margaret of Anjou' and the 'Siege of Berwick' (which ran for five nights at Covent Garden). These have as much similarity to Shakespeare's history plays as Strawberry Hill gothick has to Lincoln Cathedral. It is perhaps no coincidence that Horace Walpole thought Edward's verses 'charming'. His engaging, slightly dotty, literary mannerisms came across best in his letters, such as the lines he wrote to his niece Charlotte at her convent school in Paris: 'There is a very pretty child two doors from this house [Grosvenor Square] who was bit by a mad dog yesterday; the remedy which was given him immediately will it is hoped prevent any bad consequences: I think in a Convent you are in no danger of Mad Dogs however take care you are not bit by a Mad-Bug.'[10] On another occasion he described a bachelor dinner party as an 'assembly of virgins'; even the host's tom cat 'they assured me had never been out of the cloister'. In a later letter to Charlotte in 1807 he wrote :

> Dear Divinity,
>   I must have recourse to you in all my Difficulties – I left a pair of shoes at your House – and I am now a slip-shod old sybil instead of a veteran Bard – I should be much obliged if you could contrive to convey the children of Crispin to me.
>   Yours in great haste
>   Your Devoted Bare-footed
>   Bard.[11]

Fanny Burney, who met 'the Poet' in Bath in April 1780, left a perceptive account of his effeminate character: 'we met Mr Jerningham, the poet. I have been reading his poems, if *his* they may be called. He seems a mighty delicate gentleman: looks to be painted and all is daintification in manner speech and dress ... He sings to his own accompaniment upon the harp. He has about as much voice as Sacchini and very sweet-toned, though very English; and he sang and played with a fineness that somewhat resembled the man we looked at Piozzi's benefit; for it required a painful attention to hear him.'

Miss Burney, while unimpressed by his poetry and singing, was nevertheless touched by his kindness and 'gentle style of raillery'. When he teased her: 'Why do you take up a book Miss Burney? You know you can't read,' she replied in the same style, 'I only do it to make believe'. The Poet's niece, Charlotte, on various occasions, also noted his good-natured civility, gentleness and kindness. When he was walking in the village at Costessey, he always stopped to talk to all the inhabitants he met in the road, asking after their children and health, an unusual courtesy. John Taylor, grandson of George II's oculist and an habitué of London's literary salons, described 'the Poet' as 'a warm sincere, and steady friend, one of the most amiable characters I ever knew'. Even Byron, who could not normally resist biting the friendly hand, refrained from criticism in this case because 'he was one of the few who treated me with kindness when a boy'.[12]

He was regarded as a useful and helpful patron by a large circle of acquaintances who took advantage of his kindness of heart and wide connections to ask for favours. His correspondence is full of applications for assistance: young men seeking commissions in the army, authors trying to find publishers, actresses looking for engagements, musicians asking for recommendations, fashionable hostesses asking him to sing to his harp or recite (or even write) poems for them, and clergy cadging for preferment and posts. As an old man, however, he was already seen as a relic of vanished Georgian frivolity. Henry Crabbe Robinson in 1811, a year before 'the Poet' died, wrote: 'Mr Jerningham was present and she [Mrs Buttler, their hostess] called him to his face the last of the Old School – He is already forgotten more completely than those will be whom his friends and contemporaries treated so contemptuously.' Nevertheless, he made it into the *Dictionary of National Biography.*

All the Jerninghams seem to have been likeable characters, Frances Lady Jerningham above all. Her daughter Charlotte (who preserved 12 volumes of her mother's letters to her) paints an attractive picture. The letters, too, are redolent of Lady Jerningham's self-deprecating humour: 'Mr Lawker has published his life in two volumes. He mentions me having even in <u>declining years</u> Intelligence and Spirit …!'[13] Or her habit of addressing her letters in the winter from 'Cossey or Lapland' or when the nuns were staying *en route* for Norwich 'This Little Convent'. She was disarmingly natural and straightforward. On a visit to the opera she mentioned that William Pitt, the Prime Minister, was in their box 'which was a greater treat to my curiosity than the actress'. She also had a very nice line in neat put-downs when describing their friends and acquaintances. Lady Mulgrave's baby boy was 'healthy' but 'highly ugly at the moment' and Sir Thomas Webb was 'uncommonly fatiguing from his frothy volubility', while she wrote ironically of Charles Townley (the lapsed Catholic collector of antique marbles) 'he had too much wit to pray'. Sir William and Lady Homan – he thin, she bedaubed with artificial makeup – were nicknamed 'lath and plaster'. Her letters to Charlotte at school in Paris are unrestrainedly affectionate. In 1784 Charlotte went away to school (aged 14) but not to the English convent of the Blue Nuns in the Rue de Charenton, though it was then a most fashionable 18th-century girls' school for the English Catholics, and one where there were many family connections. Lady Mary

52 The Jerningham family in the drawing room at Costessey, one of many charming sketches by Charlotte Jerningham. Her father, Sir William, is seated behind the fire screen.

Stafford Howard, Sir William's grandmother, for instance, had been one of the first year's intake there in 1733, and his cousin Lady Anastasia Stafford Howard was a member of the Order. Frances Jerningham had herself been educated there. She chose for Charlotte, however, not an English but a French convent, the Ursulines in the Rue St Jacques, in order that she would learn better French, a good choice as Charlotte was happy there and always revered the memory of the nuns and their beautiful religious services. On 15 August 1785, she wrote to her brother Edward: 'Today is the Assumption which is the feast of the School; we have recreation for three days, our School is ornamented with flowers, relicks and all lighted up, we have a very fine alter [*sic*] at one end. That is for a <u>Salve</u> that is: hymns in honour of the Blessed Virgin, which we sing in parts accompanied by the harp.'[14]

Sir William and Frances took Charlotte to Paris themselves and Lady Jerningham began a regular correspondence with her daughter even before her carriage had started on its homeward journey: 'How does my poor Dear Little Girl do to-day? I have been awake all night thinking of you and regretting you. But I hope you will apply so well to all your masters that I shall, next summer twelve months, rejoice in the courage we both have had in parting … Papa sends his love and I join mine with a thousand kisses.'[15] No Victorian stiff upper lip there.

As well as their daughter Charlotte, the Jerninghams had three sons: George, William and Edward (Ned). The elder two were also educated on the continent, at a

French Oratorian School at Juilly rather than one of the English academies. This unusual choice of French schools for their children illustrates the Jerningham's strong Francophile tastes and connections. George was the heir and succeeded his father as 7th Baronet and became in due course the 8th Baron Stafford. William followed a military career first in the Austrian service and then, during the Napoleonic Wars, in the British army. Edward was his mother's favourite and became a barrister and a leading light in the late 18th-century campaign for Catholic Emancipation. He was also a talented amateur architect who was the moving force behind the late Georgian restoration of Stafford Castle.

On her return to London from Paris after leaving Charlotte at the Ursulines, Lady Jerningham described how Edward came to greet her. 'This day my Dearest, Dear Little Boy Neddy came here to lodge in Grosvenor Square, and looks most beautifully, his hair quite long over his eyes and his teeth very clean, with an immense colour in his cheeks. We both cryed when we met, but he is now in good spirits …'[16]

Intelligent, spirited, witty, soft-hearted, Lady Jerningham dominates the late Georgian family circle. Sir William by contrast is a more muted figure, managing his estates and trying to balance the family finances which were much stretched by the London houses in Grosvenor Square (and later in Bolton Row) and the continental education of his children. Lady Jerningham noted, 'We are not yet very affluent, Sir William finds it a good deal.'[17] Despite the many calls on his finances, he was able to undertake a number of improvements, as his rental income increased by careful management, building at Costessey a model farm and new stables to the design of Sir John Soane in 1784, and modernising the interior of the Hall, inserting sash windows and redecorating the rooms in a fashionable neo-classical taste, in 1785, with wallpaper and painted furniture. His portrait, now at Swynnerton, shows him holding one of his own architectural drawings with a Gothick tower in the background, which he built in the park at Costessey.

He was a sensible, moderate, tolerant man, and kept on good terms with his Anglican neighbours, especially the Bishop of Norwich whom he allowed to hold dances at Costessey when such frivolously non-clerical entertainments would have been inappropriate in the Bishop's Palace. Lady Jerningham describes one such occasion to Charlotte in a letter, which also alluded to the new Francophile decorations in the Tudor rooms at old Costessey. 'The dance was in the parlour, new painted and the white paper in it with a green border … the supper was in the Hall … Cards in the library … The supper at 12, the company parted at 3.'[18] Handsome Sir William comes across as good-natured, and easy going; and he shouldered his wife's enthusiasms and extravagances with patient good humour. Louis XV described him when young as *le bel Jerningham* and *le plus honnête homme que je connaie*. In his later years he was happiest farming, planting trees and shooting partridges in Norfolk, his dashing French youth firmly in the past, mixing easily with his county neighbours and tenantry, and pursuing his own enthusiasms as an amateur architect.

He was a good man of business, and the increased prosperity of the family owed much to his efficient modern farming at Costessey and the entrepreneurial development of the coal and iron in the Shropshire estates. The manors of Shifnall and Wrockwardine were in the East Shropshire coalfield, one of the pioneering areas of the Industrial Revolution with the development of the iron industry in Coalbrookdale.[19] The Jerninghams encouraged industrial development on their lands there and the increased revenue from mineral royalties from this Midlands estate helped to underpin the increasingly neo-feudal, Catholic revival at rural Costessey itself, which was to reach its romantic apotheosis in the next generation with the revival of the Stafford peerage and the Gothic reconstruction of the house.

Charlotte Jerningham's education in Paris was completed in November 1786, leaving her accomplished in French and Italian and proficient in history, music, dancing and drawing.[20] She was a spirited draughtsman and sketches by her of her classroom, contemporaries and the nuns survive. The Jerninghams went to collect her, spending some months in France, before returning home in 1787. Two years later the French Revolution broke out. The Jerningham and Dillon relations and their French friends and connections were grievously affected by the subsequent catastrophe.

53 Sir William Jerningham's pigs at the Home Farm, Costessey. Sir William was a keen farmer who developed his estates. Painting by George Morland.

54 Sir William Jerningham in the park at Costessey, showing the tower built to his own design and his sheep. Painted by Philip Reinagle.

55 The Hon. Frances (Dillon), Lady Jerningham, wife of Sir William, and a prolific letter writer, nicknamed 'Her Most Catholic Majesty' by her family.

General Arthur Dillon was guillotined in 1793. Another cousin, Theobald Dillon, was murdered by his own soldiers at Lille. Many others, including Lady Jerningham's aged uncle the Archbishop of Narbonne, emigrated to England in 1793. The 'Chevalier' Jerningham also escaped to London after the attack on the Tuilleries when the Swiss Guard were massacred. The Blue Nuns also crossed the Channel, except for Lady Anastasia Stafford Howard, who was too old to move. Lady Dillon found herself at the centre of French emigré society in London and did her best to help all the displaced aristocrats and religious, not just relations. Costessey and her London house in Bolton Row became havens for emigré clergy. Her drawing room in town became a sort of revived *ancien régime salon*. The Blue Nuns were given temporary shelter at Costessey itself, till a house was found for them in Norwich, Lady Jerningham acting as their almoner or treasurer and raising money for them. Sir William was not entirely enthusiastic about his house being turned into a convent. Lady Jerningham told Charlotte, 'Your poor father has been a little impatient about them'.

'The Poet' visited Paris for the last time in 1792 where he met Madame de Staël, the literary phenomenon of the moment. He reported to Charlotte: '... I have addressed some verses to her which M^de de Bonfleurs has translated.' While in France he witnessed some of the atrocities of the Terror at first hand:

> The mob pass'd our window on their way to the Hotel de Brienne, three doors off: there they assembled with Flambeaux without appearing to have any settled resolution of destroying the house … During this Suspense the French *Gardes* pass'd our Door, and surprising the rioters they fell upon them in a most inhumane manner, Beating their heads with the Musket and applying the point of the Bayonet to several. One poor wretch escaping the tumult, drop'd dead at our door …[21]

Despite the times Sir William and Lady Jerningham travelled again on the continent in summer 1792, taking the waters at Spa in the Low Countries. William, their second son, was then based with the Austrian army (allies of Britain) in Flanders and the Rhineland, and was soon engaged in battle against the French. He served for several years, writing home from various camps along the Rhine. Following the Treaty of Campo Formio in 1797, which established a truce between Bonaparte and the Emperor, William the soldier returned to England. While in London, he accompanied his father to a Levee at St James' Palace in his uniform and 'look'd extremely well'. He was presented to George III but 'being an Austrian officer did not kiss the King's Hand'. In 1799 he returned to Vienna, where he nearly died of pneumonia after a treacherous winter's journey down the Danube and received the Last Rites. He recovered, however, much to the relief of his distraught parents. He went back to Austria in order to surrender his commission in the imperial service as he intended to join the British army, which he subsequently did. Though technically still illegal for Catholics to serve as officers, there was now an informal arrangement whereby experienced Catholic soldiers like William could be taken on 'by acquiescence' if they could find a commander and regiment who would turn a blind eye to their religion. William was gazetted in the 57th Regiment of Foot in 1800. It contained many Irish Catholics and so he felt at home. William in Lancashire 'says most of his Regiment are Catholicks and that St Patrick's Day Mass was positively said in the Barracks.' He particularly liked Preston, where he was posted for a time, with its Jacobite and Catholic associations. So did Edward Jerningham, who on a visit to the Gillibrands (Catholic coal owners) reported 'Lancashire is like a Catholick Country and Classical Ground for a Jacobite'.[22]

The Jerninghams frequently attended Court, both the King's Levees and the Queen's Drawing Rooms, and were favourites of George III and Queen Charlotte and other members of the Royal Family. Long-suffering Sir William, however, was not as keen on London as his wife and children. He preferred a quiet life in the country,

56 Charlotte and Edward Jerningham. Charlotte was her mother's confidante and married Sir George Bedingfeld of Oxburgh. Edward became a lawyer, secretary of the Catholic Association and an amateur architect responsible for the new chapel at Costessey and for rebuilding Stafford Castle. Portrait by John Sanders, 1778.

improving his estates and entertaining his neighbours and tenantry. 'Every year I feel more disgusted of this town,' he complained to Charlotte of London in May 1800.[23]

Charlotte, herself, tall, dark-haired and blue-eyed, married in 1795 a Catholic kinsman and neighbour in Norfolk, Sir Richard Bedingfeld of Oxburgh, and had a bevy of beautiful children who married into other Catholic families. She continued to be her mother's confidante and chief correspondent. Charlotte inherited all her parents' easy charm and talents and also a concern for the less fortunate, helping wherever she could with gifts of money and other acts of charity, including sending her chaplain from Oxburgh to those in need. She describes a harrowing incident of the sort to her mother in a letter, which reveals much of her character and the Jerningham's concern for their poorer co-religionists. Charlotte had received an 'express' at Oxburgh from Wisbech

> to say that four Irish Catholics had been convicted of murder that Morning, and they being desirous of seeing a priest of their own religion … begged Sir Richard would Immediately send his Chaplain as they were to be executed on Saturday morning. Mr Patterson went, and returned yesterday evening very much hurt at the dreadful Scene he had witnessed. *Two of the 4 died perfectly innocent!* The Sheriff and all those present are now convinced of it from their behaviour on the Scaffold … They died perfectly resigned, with every Sentiment of Piety … They were all 4 sensible men well instructed in their religion and felt the comfort of it in their last moments.[24]

George Jerningham, the eldest son and heir of Sir William, also married in 1800. His wife Frances Sulyard of Haughley Park (Suffolk) was an heiress, and her fortune was to provide much of the financial basis for the 19th-century revival of the family. The Jerninghams, however, seem to have found her somewhat cold and supercilious and were slightly wary of her at first. She lacked their spontaneous warmth, though they came round to her in due course. The boot was in fact on the other foot, and she was shy of her in-laws' superior education, worldly, easy manners and cosmopolitan aristocratic connections.

Edward (Ned), (1774-1822), the youngest son and his mother's favourite, studied law at Lincoln's Inn, after a tour of France with his tutor in 1786, and also pursued his enthusiasms for genealogy, heraldry and architecture. The latter was a trait he inherited from his father. He engaged his sister Charlotte to make sketches and paintings of coats of arms for him, and spent happy hours at the College of Arms looking at old rolls of arms and Visitation Records. A typical letter from him to Charlotte (now Lady Bedingfeld) runs: 'Plowden's chevron surpasses my Heraldic powers to describe,[25] it must be familiar to your eyes; think of the silver waiters at Cossey. I must search the Heralds office to fill the five plain shields.' His heraldic and genealogical work was inspired by collecting proofs of his family's descent for the Stafford peerage claim.

Edward was also busy as an amateur architect. He drew up plans to rebuild Stafford Castle as a picturesque castellated folly and the reconstruction began in 1811, but was never finished. His notes for rebuilding the castle still survive.[26]

Edward Jerningham himself described his plans for the restoration, which formed part of his programme for the peerage claim. 'From the rebuilding of part of Stafford Castle, it is true that the adjacent lands acquire an increased local interest and value but not as a residence for the family. The object being to restore a building which since the conquest has always been considered as annexed to the Stafford Barony. It was principally on the ground of hereditary possession of this Castle that the son of the Duke of Buckingham petitioned that the Barony be restored to him in the time of Edward VI. Were we to fail in our present claim arising out of the attainder of Viscount Stafford in 1680 because of any point of law, I have no doubt that possession of this castle would be part of a strong case we would still be able to bring forward for the restitution of the barony.'[27]

The ruins had been cleared of rubbish and prettily landscaped by Sir William Jerningham in 1783 after he had inherited the property, revealing and repairing the old stone walls to a height of about twelve feet. Sir William also seems to have rebuilt one of the towers as an eye-catcher and lookout. At least, a single standing tower is visible in late 18th-century views of the castle. Edward aimed to rebuild the east end of the castle to full height with two towers 60 feet high and battlements to serve as a landmark and showpiece and occasional residence. The mason was John Brown of Milford who signed the contract in 1813, and the roof was on the new work by 1817.

57 George, 8th Lord Stafford as a boy. Portrait by John Downman.

The setting was also improved, trees being planted round the motte to enhance the picturesque appearance of the place. The castle was opened to the public from the 1820s onwards with a resident caretaker who showed visitors round. The reconstructed building contained a 'banqueting hall' on the first floor resplendent with Stafford heraldry, oak panelling, armour and a miscellany of 'curious antiquities'. The recon-struction of Stafford Castle was an interesting demonstration of late Georgian attitudes towards ancient buildings, which in turn foreshadowed the modern restoration and public display of such monuments.

Edward Jerningham also designed a magnificent private chapel in the Perpendicular Gothic style at Costessey, part inspired by that at King's College Cambridge The interior was vaulted (in plaster), and the windows filled with a fine collection of medieval English and continental stained glass which gave the chapel a genuine aura of ancient Catholic piety. Sadly, it was to be first used publicly for Sir William's requiem mass. He died in 1809. Edward had invited Bishop Milner to dedicate the chapel, and this took place the day before the funeral.

Edward's principal public achievement was his role as the Secretary of the Catholic Board, a body of leading Catholic clergy and laity campaigning for Catholic Emancipation which succeeded the ineffective Cisalpine Club, a group of Whiggish Catholic gentry. He successfully master-minded the steps towards Emancipation in these years, organising petitions to the Crown and lobbying peers and M.P.s. In 1820 he organised a petition signed by 20,000 Catholics, which was presented by the Duke of Norfolk to George IV after his accession to the throne, and was involved with Canning's ineffective bill to allow the Catholic peers to sit in the House of Lords. With his legal expertise and antiquarian enthusiasms, Edward was also the driving force behind the Jerningham family's attempt to retrieve the Stafford barony, from 1809 onwards, and this went hand in hand with the Emancipation campaign in Edward's office. Edward was one of a group of English Catholic aristocrats including Lord Petre and Bernard Howard (heir to and, after 1815, 12th Duke of Norfolk) who were extremely active in the second half of George III and George IV's reigns in their attempts to reinstate Catholics into the mainstream of public life, and this also formed part of the official policy of the Grenville faction of the Whig party. Campaigns were organised, petitions signed and presentations made to the King and the Prime Minister. One by one various minor concessions were made and finally in 1829 full emancipation for Catholics was achieved. Edward Jerningham was tireless in his efforts to co-ordinate these petitions and to unite the disparate Catholic groupings and interests into an integrated campaign.[28]

The death of Lady Anastasia Stafford Howard in Paris in 1807 made Sir William the *de facto* 7th Lord Stafford, if the attainder could be reversed, and this Edward now set about achieving. He was to be successful in this, as also in preparing the way for Catholic Emancipation, though he himself did not live to see either, dying prematurely of erysipelas while still under fifty. At the same time in 1822 his wife and their maid also died of the same contagious febrile illness, a tragedy that overwhelmed his aged mother and overcast the Jerningham's final achievement of the family coronet.

VIII

The Revival of the Stafford Peerage

∽·∾

'THE GRAND AFFAIR of the <u>Title</u> must be commenced', wrote Lady Jerningham to Charlotte (Lady Bedingfeld) in May 1807.

> The Dear Lawyer in our Family [Edward] says that it turns solely upon one question: The Viscount Stafford and the Heiress having been first created Baron and Baroness Stafford for them and their Heirs. There is not a doubt of its having comprehended the female line and that conveys the Honour directly to your Father. But Lord Stafford's Blood was contaminated by the attainder. Query: Could his Wife <u>solely</u> convey the Peerage – when the creation was to Both and their posterity. It must be decided upon, tho' it is a bad moment for to Revert to Popery and to the injustice that has been done in former Reigns from that foolish cry … Hargrave says that your Father is Earl of Hereford, Essex, Stafford etc. If we get the Barony it will do very well for the present.[1]

The formal petition for the peerage was printed and presented to the House of Lords in May 1808. The view of the Committee of Privileges which dealt with peerage claims, however, was that the title could not be inherited solely from Mary Viscountess Stafford and that, if the title were to be restored, the easiest path was to apply for an Act of Parliament to reverse Viscount Stafford's attainder which was everywhere recognised as an instance of gross injustice. The Duke of Norfolk, head of the Howard family, advised Edward that it would be as 'easy as a Turnpike Bill'.

Though the campaign for the title in earnest only got underway after Lady Anastasia's death in 1807, Sir William had opened the case as early as 1800 when he had written to William Pitt, the Prime Minister, putting the claim of Lady Anastasia and himself to the Stafford Barony with legal counsel's opinion. The case was to be successfully concluded in favour of his eldest son George in 1824. The initial case ran from 1810 to 1814 when the Committee of Privileges of the House of Lords accepted Sir George's descents and claims but ruled that the attainder would have to be reversed. There was never any problem with the Stafford-Howard Jerningham pedigree. The Attorney General, Sir Vicary Gibbs, had accepted Sir William's proof of descent as early as 1808.

Edward's scheme for reversing the attainder was to get all the Howard peers, led by the Duke of Norfolk, to address the King to ask His Majesty to revoke the great injustice done to 'their Relative Viscount Stafford'. This was agreed to, and The Duke of Norfolk, The Earl of Suffolk and Berkshire, The Earl of Carlisle and Lord Howard of Effingham sent a formal petition to the King from 'We the undersigned Heads of the House of Howard', asking the Crown to rectify the situation. The Duke of Norfolk immediately received a letter from the Secretary of State saying that 'His Majesty had ordered that one of the Privy Council should convey to the House of Peers his desire of having the attainder removed from Sir William Howard, Viscount Stafford.' A bill to this effect passed through both houses of Parliament and received the Royal Assent on 17 June 1824:

> Whereas it is just and proper that the said Attainder should be reversed: Be it therefore enacted … that the said Conviction, Attainder and Judgement … against the said William late Viscount Stafford, are hereby reversed, repealed, revoked, annulled and made utterly void to all Intents and Purposes as if the same had never been.

In 1825 Sir George Jerningham received a writ of summons to Parliament as 8th Baron Stafford. He had hoped that he might have received the peerage in time to attend the coronation of George IV in 1821. He was four years too late for that, but he and his family were nevertheless very pleased.[2] The reversal of the Stafford attainder was among a number of political manoeuvres that were used to test the ground for full-scale Catholic Emancipation which was finally achieved in 1829. In the same year as the repeal of the attainder, the Duke of Norfolk himself had introduced a bill (which was successfully passed with the support of the Whigs) to allow him to exercise the Duties of Earl Marshal though a Catholic. The Stafford Attainder Bill fitted into this pattern. Its successful repeal enabled Sir William Jerningham to inherit the Stafford barony, though not yet take his seat in the House of Lords. (He would have to wait until 1829 for that when the Catholic Emancipation Bill was finally passed by Wellington and Peel.)

An appropriately feudal reception was arranged for the arrival of the new Lord and Lady Stafford at Costessey.

> Lord and Lady Stafford returned to Costessy after officially obtaining the barony … their horses were replaced by 30 men dressed with sashes and other decorations. They were headed by as many as 150 horsemen riding in pairs, with a band and 100 children carrying banners and flags,

58 George Stafford
Jerningham, 8th Lord
Stafford. He
successfully claimed the
title in 1825. Portrait by
Daniel Gardner.

59 Frances (Sulyard), wife of the 8th Lord
Stafford, 'the most beautiful in person, the most
powerful in mind, the most commanding,
graceful and attractive in manners'. Portrait by
Michael Archer Shee.

60 The Duke of Sussex, friend of the
Jerninghams and regular visitor to Costessey. He
gave this portrait by Chester Harding to the 8th
Lord Stafford in 1828.

61 Stafford Castle as rebuilt by Edward Jerningham to his own design in 1813-17. (Salt Library, Stafford)

etc. Church bells and more cannon volleys greeted their arrival … Lord and Lady Stafford gave each parishioner as well as children: 1 lb. of meat, a twopenny loaf and a pint of beer. For general consumption, there was in addition a fat bullock and a half, 3 sheep 800 twopenny loaves and as many pints of beer as they could accommodate.[3]

The new peer, George Stafford, and his wife, Frances, had more permanent plans for celebrating the restoration of the barony: the reconstruction of Costessey Hall on a grandiose scale to create a suitably neo-feudal demonstration of the Jerningham's new lordly status. His wife was as enthusiastic about this architectural project as he was, which was just as well as it was her fortune that was to be expended in this way, her family estate at Haughley having been sold for the purpose. Lady Stafford took a keen interest in the details of the design of the new house, and made notes on visits to country houses recording the dimensions of the principal rooms and other features that pleased her for imitation in the new work at Costessey. The generous sizes of the new reception rooms, for instance, at Costessey were her idea.

The large new wings were got underway immediately in 1826. Lord and Lady Stafford chose as their architect John Chessel Buckler (1793-1894), a celebrated topographical artist who specialised in medieval and Tudor architecture. The Stafford family were his major patrons for, apart form Costessey, they employed him to design a new Catholic church and school at Shifnall on the Shropshire estate, and Charlotte's

62 J.C. Buckler's design for the reconstruction of the entrance side of Costessey Park, 1828.

63 J.C. Buckler's view of Costessey Park from across the River Tud, with the new service court on the left, 'Grand Tower' in the centre, and Edward Jerningham's Catholic Chapel on the right.

eldest son, Sir Henry Bedingfeld, employed him to re-edify Oxburgh Hall and to design a new, detached private chapel there. Buckler also produced unexecuted designs for a huge house in Scotland for Charlotte Bedingfeld's daughter, Charlotte Georgiana, and her husband Thomas Fraser, later Lord Lovat.

At Costessey, the new work comprised vast additions in Tudor Gothic style with a large square tower, turrets, gables, and myriad twisted brick chimney stacks. The old estate brickyard was developed specially to produce the ornamental brickwork to Buckler's design for the new building, notably the decorative chimney stacks. The Costessey brickyard continued in commercial production throughout the 19th century and its products were well-known as Cosseyware; they can still be found on many 19th-century buildings in Norfolk.[4]

Some of Buckler's designs for Costessey and lists of his sources for various features survive and show his delight in adapting genuine Tudor and medieval details: chimneys and finials from East Elsingham Hall, Barsham Manor and Thornbury Castle; rainwater heads, battlements, bay windows and gables from Oxford colleges,

64 Costessey: The Chapel Corridor copied from Christ Church, Oxford, by J.C. Buckler.

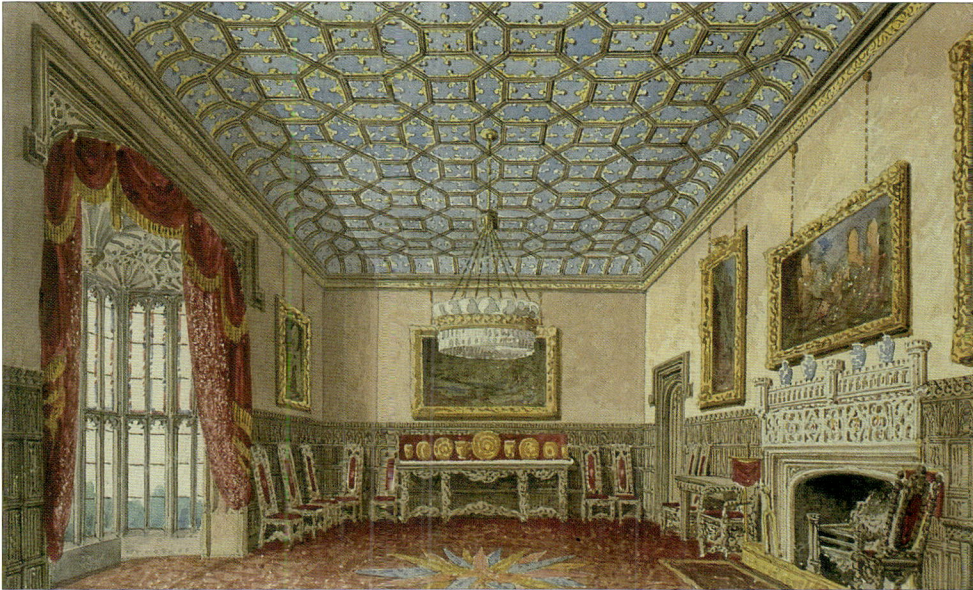

65 Costessey: The Dining Room, 1826, by J.C. Buckler.

66 Costessey: The Drawing Room, 1826 by J.C. Buckler.

67 Costessey: the
Gallery, by J.C. Buckler.

Hengrave, Compton Wynyates, Melford, Great Chalfield, Layer Marney, Hampton Court and other famous historic buildings. The results according to J.C. Loudon in his *Encyclopaedia of Cottage, Farm and Villa Architecture (1833)* made Costessey 'the richest Gothic building in England'. It was certainly among the most remarkable of English Romantic revival buildings. The archaeological accuracy of the detail and the heraldic display foreshadowed the Palace of Westminster and other Victorian buildings.

Though the work went on for nearly three decades, the house was never completed and plans to build a large Great Hall and to replace the Tudor house, itself with new ranges, were never carried out. The result was that the old house survived, dwarfed by the encircling wings and towers of Buckler's late Georgian Tudor revival architecture. The new tower was 150 feet high. When the design was shown at the Royal Academy in 1833 it was described as 'the complete revival of ancient English architecture which may be witnessed in this fine seat. The entire design shows a mansion which even Sir Reginald Bray or Cardinal Wolsey might have acknowledged.' The new rooms were furnished in suitably romantic style with old oakwork bought in London, and arms and armour acquired through Sir Richard Meyrick, the great expert on armour who arranged the arms at Windsor Castle and the Tower of London and whose own house at Goodrich Court (Herefordshire) was a positive museum of old armour.[5] The assemblage of treasures redolent of 'antique magnificence' was one of the key attributes of Costessey: medieval stained glass, portraits, books, manuscripts and Stafford family relics of all descriptions.[6]

68 Costessey Park, showing the old house alongside the Buckler additions. (NMR)

69 Costessey Park: Buckler's new drawing room and dining room and the Grand Tower. (NMR)

70 Charlotte, Lady Bedingfeld, as a
widow and Lady in Waiting to
Queen Adelaide.

Lady Stafford did not live long to enjoy the magnificent new mansion which she and her husband had created. She died in 1831 and was buried in the Catholic chapel at Costessey. 'We are met together … to lament in the holy temple of God … all that this world now possesses of that noble and exalted Lady, who so lately walked before us in all the majesty of rank and all the dignity of virtue …', as the family chaplain, the Revd F.C. Husenbeth, preached at her funeral.[7]

The family circle was beginning to contract. Old Lady Jerningham had died in 1825. Charlotte's husband, Sir Richard Bedingfeld, had died in the winter of 1830, and she had entered the Catholic Convent at Hammersmith as a widow-pensioner, not as a nun. She had her own sitting room there full of family portraits and mementoes. She liked the peace at Hammersmith: 'There is something in the Strict Order and Control of a Religious House which is wise and salutary – I should never have gained as much ground in the way of Resignation elsewhere.' She found visits to the Jerninghams' London house in Bolton Row, 'where my brother Edward's Wit and my dear Mother's conversation amused and delighted all', to be a sad experience now, without them.

She did not pine, however, and was to have an interesting old age. When William IV ascended the throne in 1830, his consort Queen Adelaide of Saxe Meiningen was an old acquaintance of Charlotte's from the time after the end of the Napoleonic Wars, when their respective families had spent the winters in Ghent. The new Queen appointed Charlotte a Woman of the Bedchamber. So she alternated between her cosy room at the Hammersmith Convent and the gilded splendours of Windsor Castle, where she attended the Queen at Royal Drawing Rooms, balls and state visits of foreign royalties. She appreciated the contrasts in her life between 'the little humble convent and the magnificence and splendour of Golden Windsor' which 'sets me moralising'. She continued in the Queen's household till Queen Adelaide's death in 1849.

The Jerninghams had been friends of the French and English Royal families throughout the late 18th and early 19th centuries. Sir William and his wife Frances had been favourites of George III and Queen Charlotte. Edward 'the Poet' was a crony of the Prince Regent's at Carlton House and Brighton Pavilion. Several of the royal dukes were personal friends. The pro-Catholic Duke of Sussex visited Costessey from Holkham in 1819 to shoot with Sir George (soon to be Lord Stafford). He was greeted with 'God Save the King' in the chapel where he duly admired 'the beautiful stained glass'. The Duke of Gloucester came in 1832 when Henry Bedingfeld, Charlotte's eldest son who had inherited his grandmother's sense, thought the royal guest 'rather foolish and prosing'. This familiarity helped to smooth the way for the restoration of the peerage, and was one of the elements which helped to prepare for full Catholic Emancipation in 1829.

Edward, the Secretary of the Catholic Board, was a staunch *legitimist*, devoted to the Stuarts and the Bourbons. He called his sons Charles Edward and James Stuart after Bonnie Prince Charlie and the Old Pretender. He spent much time hobnobbing with Louis XVIII and the French Court while they were in English exile, and accompanied the King to Paris after the first defeat of Napoleon in 1814. He was a friend of all the French royal family and what old Lady Jerningham jokingly called the 'courtisans'. Louis XVIII was touched by his support and gave him a gold box with the royal miniature framed in diamonds.

The French connections and interests of the family lasted well into the 19th century. Edward's grandson, Sir Hubert Edward Henry Jerningham (1842-1914), a distinguished diplomat, began his career in Paris as attaché during the embassy of Lord Lyons to the Emperor Napoleon III. There he was popular in French literary circles and the houses of the old *noblesse* in the Faubourg St Germain. He was especially fond of the sister of the Duc de Broglie, Mme d'Haussonville (grand-daughter of Mme de Staël whom Edward the Poet had admired in Paris in 1792). He thought she 'possessed all that can make life agreeable without any of the drawbacks whatsoever. She was clever, handsome, well read, rich.' She gave him her two works on Byron, *La Jeunesse* and *Les Dernières Années*. Hubert Jerningham himself was not without literary gifts. He translated the *Recollections of Lord Byron* by La Marquise de Boissy, the poems of Heine, and wrote a couple of volumes of memoirs of his years in France: *Reminiscences of an Attaché* (1870) and *Life in A French Chateau* (1866).

He left Paris in 1870 at the time of the French defeat and fall of Napoleon III. His exceptional mastery of the French language (he, like his 18th-century ancestors, had been educated in Paris where he had obtained a degree from the Sorbonne) continued to be of use to the British Government in the West Indies, where many of the islands, under British rule since the Napoleonic wars were still French-speaking. He was Colonial Secretary at Honduras 1887-9, Minister, Lieutenant Governor and then Governor of Mauritius from 1889 to 1897, and finally Governor of Trinidad and Tobago from 1897-1900. He was also M.P. for Berwick on Tweed from 1881 to 1885. His wife, Annie Liddall, came from Northumberland, and he acquired his own country house there – Longridge Tower – which he rebuilt to the design of the long-lived J.C. Buckler, who had designed the enlargement of Costessey in the 1820s and 1830s.

Sir Hubert Jerningham was one of two notable diplomats in the family in the 19th century. The other was George Sulyard Stafford Jerningham (1806-74), the third son of George, Lord Stafford. He was educated at Oscott, the Catholic college near Birmingham. Between 1830 and 1872 he was posted to various British embassies in the European capitals. His first job was at The Hague where he was appointed Secretary at the Legation. His time coincided with the breakaway of Belgium from Holland and the establishment of an independent kingdom under British protection, which made the English unpopular in Holland. Subsequently, he was appointed Secretary at the Legation to the King of Sardinia (Turin) 1836, then at the Embassy to the Queen of Portugal (Lisbon) in 1837 and Plenipotentiary at the latter embassy in 1838. He was Secretary to the Embassy to the Queen of Spain (Madrid) from 1839, and at Paris in 1850; he then served at Stockholm and Stuttgart. He kept a journal from his early 20s, partly in French and partly in English, which he called 'the register of my ideas as well as my actions'. He inherited the writing skills of his family and had a neat turn of phrase. He described the restoration of Bourbon rule in France as 'inserting a race-horse into a hay-cart'. Unusually in the Jerningham family, who were generally devoted to the memory of Louis XV and Louis XVI, he had an admiration for Napoleon. This may be because as a boy his mother had given him a bust of Napoleon. This had been confiscated by the Customs on its import into England and then rescued from a fire at the Customs House and bought by her at a sale of damaged artefacts.

He returned home from The Hague for Christmas 1831 which he spent with the family of Costessey. He described the traditional programme with midnight mass in the chapel, followed by fried sausages for supper-breakfast. There was snow on the ground for weeks, much shooting partridges and pheasants, and regular strong hang-overs: 'Woke in a horrid state of head-ache … could not stir till 12 o'clock and then felt most penitent. Drinking kills me. I can start 1 or 3 bottles without immediate bad effects, but the next morning …!'[9]

Although considered the clever one of his family, George hero-worshipped his eldest brother Henry Valentine, whom he considered to be far more handsome and brilliant than himself. Henry Valentine Stafford Jerningham succeeded his father as 8th Baronet and 9th Baron Stafford. He was active in politics, and had sat in Parliament as M.P. for Pontefract from 1830 to 1834. He also continued to improve Costessey, building new Tudor-style kennels in the park and other outbuildings. He continued to use the long-lived family architect J. C. Buckler. There was a great flurry of remodelling and refurbishing in preparation for a royal visit to Costessey Hall in 1866. Following his marriage to Princess Alexandra of Denmark and acquisition of his own country

house in Norfolk at Sandringham, Edward, Prince of Wales, made a formal royal visit
to Norwich. Lord Stafford acted as his host and the royal couple stayed for three days
at Costessey Hall, which was the nearest historic seat to the city suitable for the
reception of royalty. Such a prominent mark of royal favour was greatly appreciated
by a Catholic family like the Staffords who had in the past been excluded from public
life and suffered for their faith. It marked their acceptance back into the mainstream
of English life with two M.P.s, two diplomats, a member of the Royal Household and
various officers in the army. This easy absorption back into official duties and public
activities was typical of the old Catholic families in 19th-century England.

For the royal visit, a large quantity of new furniture to Buckler's design was
ordered specially from the fashionable London cabinet-makers Holland & Son, including
new chairs with the Stafford crests emblazoned in gold on the red leather backs and
the Stafford knot carved on the front rail. The visit was a great success and Princess
Alexandra wrote Lady Stafford a thank-you letter in her own hand which was carefully
preserved: 'Sandringham, 2 November 1866. Dear Lady Stafford … Thank you for
your kindness … Touched by the loyalty of Norwich … our county.'[10]

These decorative embellishments were the overture to further work at the Hall
which marked the high point of the Jerningham Stafford family. In 1869-70 Buckler
made designs for a new wing containing rooms for Lord Stafford, a study, record room
and writing room.[11] He also made designs for a large great hall with an arch-braced
timber roof, but this was not executed. The house, by this time, was a sprawling mass
of buildings of different dates, the low ceilinged entrance hall in the old Tudor house
giving access to a vast gallery on a totally different scale furnished with old oak and
numerous antiquarian pieces, from which opened Buckler's 1826 drawing room, dining
room and library, still Georgian in their proportions but with correctly detailed
chimney pieces, door cases and ceiling patterns, showing Buckler's genius for authentic
Gothic which foreshadowed Pugin's work at the Palace of Westminster and made the
house a suitable reflection of the restored Stafford peerage with all its historical
associations. It is sad that it was nearly totally demolished between the Wars, after the
Jerninghams died out, and that so many of the historic heirlooms assembled there have
been dispersed, beginning with the sale of the library in 1885.[12]

The royal visit marked the high point of 19th-century Costessey. Thereafter the
house was the home to a rapid succession of elderly, childless Lords Stafford who
brought an end to the Jerningham line. Although he married twice, Henry Valentine
had no children, and on his death aged 82 in 1884 he was succeeded by his 54-year-
old nephew Augustus as 10th Lord Stafford. He was unmarried, and certified mad,
and in due course, on his death 12 years later in 1892, he was succeeded by his
younger brother Fitzosbert. He was not married either and died in 1913. He was the
last of the Jerningham Lords Stafford. The story did not end there, however. The
baronetcy survived for a further generation being inherited by a cousin, Henry (1867-
1935), the son of Adolphus (grandson of William the soldier in the Napoleonic wars).
He was the 11th and last baronet and died in 1935. The barony itself passed again to

71 Emily Charlotte Jerningham, who married
Basil Fitzherbert of Swynnerton, Staffordshire,
through whom the Stafford title descended to
that family. Portrait by Richard Buckner.

72 Basil Fitzherbert of Swynnerton. Portrait by
Edward Taylor, 1864.

the heir general through the female line and was inherited by Francis Fitzherbert of
Swynnerton, Staffordshire, together with some portraits and heirlooms, and Stafford
Castle and the Shifnall estate; these two properties mark a thread of physical continuity
between the three families – Howards, Jerninghams and Fitzherberts – who have held
the Stafford barony since the 17th century. Francis Fitzherbert's mother, Emily, was
the sister of the 10th and 11th Lords Stafford and it was through her that the title
descended once again through the female line to the family which holds it today.

   Augustus and Fitzherbert and Emily were the children of Edward Jerningham, the
second son of George 8th Lord Stafford and Frances Sulyard. Edward was an army
officer and is best remembered for his participation in the Eglinton Tournament in
1839. Edward's role at the tournament, the famous recreation of medieval chivalry in
Ayrshire, was all of a piece with the revived feudalism at Costessey. He appeared in
armour as the Knight of the Swan, the Stafford crest, 'and so perfectly copied the
flight of this marvellous bird that, darting down the lists at the Railway Knight, he lost
his balance and flew into the sunshine while his horse, suddenly relieved of his
control, trampled over an innocent nearby varlet.'[13]

   Edward married Marianne Smythe, the adopted daughter of Mrs Fitzherbert, the
widow of Thomas Fitzherbert of Swynnerton and the illegal wife of George IV. This
link between the Jerningham and Fitzherbert families foreshadowed the eventual
coming together of the Stafford title and the Fitzherbert family.

IX

Mrs Fitzherbert

ॐ·ॐ

THE HON EDWARD STAFFORD JERNINGHAM, Knight of the Swan in the Eglinton Tournament, married Marianne Smythe, the famous Mrs Fitzherbert's niece and adopted daughter. This was the first connection between the Stafford-Jerninghams and the Fitzherbert family of Swynnerton, but relations between the two families were to grow increasingly close in the course of the 19th century with the marriage of Edward and Marianne's daughter Emily to Basil Thomas Fitzherbert, and eventually the Stafford barony was to be inherited in 1913 by the Fitzherberts as heirs general to the 11th and last Jerningham Lord Stafford.

Mrs Fitzherbert (who made their name famous) was a Fitzherbert by marriage only. She married Thomas Fitzherbert (as her second husband) in 1778 at St George's, Hanover Square. He inherited Swynnerton in autumn of the same year. They were only married for three years and Thomas died in 1781 of a contagious illness of the lungs (tuberculosis) thought at the time to have been brought on by having a bath after his strenuous exertions during the Gordon Riots. They had gone to Nice for his health, but to no avail and she was left a widow for the second time.

They had no living children (their only child died in infancy), and Thomas Fitzherbert was succeeded by his brother Basil so there is no family descent directly from her, though she treated Marianne, her adopted daughter as her co-heiress, and so several of her possessions descended to the Stafford family.

Mrs Fitzherbert was born in 1756 Mary Anne (Maria) Smythe, daughter of Walter Smythe and niece of Sir John Smythe of Acton Burnall in Shropshire (a recusant Catholic family). Her mother was an Errington from Northumberland, and her father was the half-brother of the formerly Catholic Earl of Sefton. Despite her aristocratic connections she grew up in comparatively modest circumstances at Bambridge in Hampshire, one of six children of a younger son of a Catholic family. She was reasonably well-educated, however, and like Charlotte Jerningham (Lady Bedingfeld) was a pupil at a convent in France, where she acquired perfect French and a cosmopolitan

73 Maria Smythe, Mrs Fitzherbert, wife of George IV.

finish. Her school was not in Paris but at Dunkirk. While in France she visited Versailles where she saw Louis XV dine in public; the King had sent the pretty English girl a present of sugar plums from his table. She was good-looking if not a great beauty. Her nose was too equiline – her family teased her about her 'Roman Catholic nose' – but she had a good 'white rose' complexion and an animated, unaffected manner that people found very attractive. Lady Hester Stanhope (the eccentric niece of William Pitt) wrote that Mrs Fitzherbert was one of those people 'who are sweet by nature and who even if they are not washed for a fortnight are free from odour'.

In 1775 at the age of 18 she married the 34-year-old Edward Weld of Lulworth Castle in Dorset, a Catholic widower, but he died from a fall from his horse a few months after the marriage. Then followed her short-lived marriage to Thomas Fitzherbert from 1778 to 1781. All this was perfectly conventional behaviour for a young Catholic woman of her background and education. What happened next was extraordinary.

74 Thomas Fitzherbert of Swynnerton, Maria's second husband. Portrait by George Knapton.

A year or two after her second marriage, while they were driving in Park Lane (near their London house), Thomas Fitzherbert had said, 'Look, there is the Prince' and she saw for the first time the 18-year-old heir to the throne (as she herself told George Dawson-Damer in 1836). The Fitzherberts saw the Prince again a few days later when they were on their way to a party at the Townleys. This time she realised that the Prince of Wales had followed her and stopped to look at her. They did not meet on that occasion.

After her husband's death in 1781 Maria Fitzherbert lived quietly as a widow for a couple of years, mainly on the continent, until the Earl and Countess of Sefton persuaded her to come out of her widowhood and to take part in the London Season under their protection. *The Morning Herald* announced in March 1784: 'Mrs Fitzherbert is arrived in London for the Season.' The Seftons were Whigs and their circle included such leading lights as Charles James Fox and The Duchess of Devonshire. Maria was soon swept up in the thick of fashionable Whig society which revolved around the Prince of Wales at Carlton House.

She met the Prince, most appropriately, at the opera to which she had gone with her uncle, Henry Errington. At the end of the performance the Prince had come up to Errington and said, 'Who the devil is that pretty girl you have on your arm Henry?'. Errington told him and introduced the Prince to Mrs Fitzherbert. She was 28, he was 22. The Prince fell in love with her. He was handsome and charming and his strong defects of character were not yet too apparent. He went to extraordinary lengths to win her, with extravagant solicitations, tears and hysterics. He followed her. He insisted that she was invited to the same parties as himself. He besieged her house in Park Street talking of love 'celestial and eternal'. As she herself later described it, 'The

75 The Prince Regent. Portrait by Sir Joshua Reynolds (Arundel Castle)

Prince exerted himself to his utmost to please her, and his utmost was very good indeed'.

Mrs Fitzherbert was aware of the social advantage of a connection with the Prince but was determined not to become his mistress. The Prince involved all London, including the Duchess of Devonshire, who recorded: 'upon coming to town [from Bath] many circumstances had thrown me into unfortunate intimacy with him, and he would not rest till he told me his passion for Mrs F. and his design to marry her; any remonstrance from me was always followed by threats of killing himself.' Much alarmed, The Duchess visited Mrs Fitzherbert at her own house and was re-assured when 'she agreed with me in the impossibility of his ideas; and her good sense and resolution seemed so strong that I own I felt secure in her never giving way…'

The climax came on the night of 8 July 1784 when the Prince staged a histrionic suicide attempt, by lightly stabbing himself. That evening at bedtime a posse of Carlton House courtiers arrived at Maria's house – Lord Southampton, Lord Onslow, Edward Bouverie and the Prince's Surgeon 'in the utmost consternation'. The Prince had stabbed himself and was tearing off his bandages. 'Only *her* immediate presence would save him.' At first she refused to go, but she was won over by their concern

76 Miniature by Richard Cosway of the Prince Regent, given to Mrs Fitzherbert.

and finally agreed on condition that she was accompanied by The Duchess of Devonshire. The Duchess left a record of the incident:

> I consented and traversed the court [of Devonshire House] where I found her in her chariot, and we went to Carlton House where we found the Prince in bed, his wound still bleeding. He extorted from her some promise of marriage and we left him … Mrs F. own'd to me her having given this extorted consent which she looked upon as such and in consequence we drew up and signed the inclos'd paper and she went abroad immediately.

The Duchess's statement ended, 'promises obtain'd in such a manner are entirely void G. Devonshire, M. Fitzherbert.'

Mrs Fitzherbert had already been planning to travel on the continent with her friend Lady Anne Lindsay (daughter of the Earl of Balcarres) before this crisis. Mrs Fitzherbert left for the continent the day following the Carlton House 'suicide' attempt with Lady Anne, who kept a journal describing their itinerary and conversations, and was away from England for a year, travelling in France, Holland and Germany. The Prince was in despair. He wrote her an 18-page letter the next day signed 'not only the most affectionate of lovers but the tenderest of husbands'. Letter after letter followed her from Paris to Spa, to Holland, to the Swiss Alps, to Lorraine. She tried to reassure him with a written promise 'never to marry any other person'. By autumn 1785 she had come to a decision and she let it be known that she might marry him. She had only known older husbands, 'honest country squires'. The Prince was young and glamorous. She gave in perhaps out of a mixture of love and social ambition. She was genuinely in love with him and such a marriage represented a sharp rise up the social ladder. Lady Anne Lindsay's Journal shows that she was not without social ambition.

The proposed marriage was illegal under the 1772 Royal Marriages Act, which forbade members of the Royal Family to marry without the King's permission. Even more seriously, the terms of the Act of Settlement (1701) rendered it impossible for an heir to inherit the throne if he married a Catholic. There was general unease. Charles James Fox put the arguments against the marriage in a beautifully written letter to the Prince:

> A marriage with a Catholic throws the Prince contracting such Marriage out of succession to the Crown … Surely, Sir, this is not a matter to be trifled with … It will be said that a woman who had lived with you as your wife, without being so, is not fit to be Queen of England. A mock Marriage (for it can be no other) is neither honourable for any of the parties, nor with respect to your Royal Highness, even safe. This appears so clear to me that, if I were Mrs Fitzherbert's father or brothers I would advise her not by any means to agree to it, and to prefer any species of connection with you to one leading to so much misery and mischief.

There was also the delicate problem of children. If an illegal royal marriage was subsequently ratified and legalised by Parliament it would illegitimise any previous children.

The Prince assured Fox that there was no truth in the rumours of a marriage. On Thursday 15 December he married Mrs Fitzherbert in the drawing room at her Park Street House. The Anglican clergyman who married them was the Revd Robert Burt, a chaplain in ordinary to the Prince of Wales, who, it is said, promised him an ecclesiastical promotion for his assistance, and possibly £500, though there is no proof of this. The Cavendishes, Fox and all those who had advised the Prince not to proceed were 'out of Town'. Her eldest brother, Wat Smythe, also refused to have anything to do with the illegal marriage. The witnesses were her uncle Henry Errington and her younger brother Jack. As far as the Catholic Church was concerned, it was a valid marriage according to Roman Canon law, despite the fact that it was illegal in English law. Mrs Fitzherbert accepted that 'according to the law in England [it] is not valid, yet a Marriage it certainly is according to every other law human and divine'.

At first the marriage was happy, and Mrs Fitzherbert enjoyed her demi-royal status. Mrs Fitzherbert kept her own house and the Prince of Wales spent the nights there, always using the formula, 'Madam, may I be allowed the honour of seeing you home in my carriage'. Wherever they went, and at Carlton House itself, he insisted on her having precedence as his wife. She took a box at the opera. She sold her house

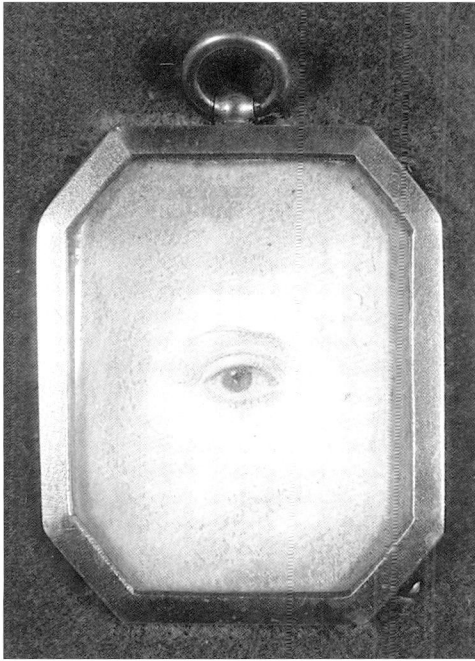

77 Miniature by Richard Cosway of the Prince Regent's eye, given to Mrs Fitzherbert.

78 Miniature of Mrs Fitzherbert by Derval.

in Park Street and bought one closer to Carlton House, in Pall Mall, which the Prince did up for her at a cost of £50,000. She also bought a house in Brighton near to the Prince's Pavilion. Their life in Brighton came closest to a domestic idyll with drives and picnics on the Downs and select suppers at the Pavilion.

Her friends and relations were puzzled and alarmed by her marriage. By the spring of 1786, the news was in the public domain. Lady Jerningham expressed the general feeling in a letter to Charlotte in March 1786:

> Mrs Fitzherbert has I believe, been married to the Prince. But it is a very hazardous undertaking as there are two acts of Parliament against the validity of such an Alliance: concerning her being a subject and her being a Catholick God knows how it will all turn out – it may be to the Glory of our Belief, or it may be to the great dismay and destruction of it! She has taken a Box to herself at the Opera which no Lady but the Dutchess of Cumberland ever did – a hundred guineas a year! The Prince is very assiduous in attending her in all public places, but she lives in her own House, and he at his.

Others were more forthright. Mrs Talbot, another Catholic, noted: 'After a while, she will be a most unhappy woman.' Rumours flew around, in particular that they had

79 Necklace given to Mrs Fitzherbert by the Prince Regent.

80 Gold and enamel snuff box given to Mrs Fitzherbert by the Prince Regent.

had children, though this was never proved and no children of the marriage are recorded. Mrs Fitzherbert later adopted two 'daughters'. The couple frequently featured in contemporary caricatures such as Gillray's brilliant 'Marriage of Figaro' (13 May 1786) or, more scurrilously, 'The Royal Toast', ''Twas Nobody saw the Lovers Leap', and 'The April Fool or Follies of the Night'. Between 1786 and 1816 the Prince's marriage to Mrs Fitzherbert featured in 127 caricatures. The marriage did great harm to the Prince's reputation, and by association to the Whigs which the Tories, naturally, made the most of. While blame and disapproval attached to the Prince, little criticism was directed towards Mrs Fitzherbert herself, who was regarded as handling a difficult imbroglio with immense tact and discretion. Her manner remained quiet and civil and she never misused her great influence. Mary Frampton noted in her diary:

> Mrs Fitzherbert's very uncomfortable life since her connection with the Prince affords as strong a lesson as was ever given in favour of virtue, for she never desired any benefit from it … Her chariot was without armorial bearings nor has she ever worn any, since her liveries by accident resembled the Royal ones, the Fitzherberts livery being red trimmed with green and … gold ornaments.

Cracks soon began to appear. Within a year of his illegal marriage the Prince's enormous and life-long debts first began to catch up with him. Questions about his rumoured marriage were asked in the House of Commons. When the Prince applied to Parliament for a special monetary grant to clear them, Fox denied that a marriage had taken place, having been personally assured, he thought, by the Prince to that effect. 'I now pronounce [the marriage] by whomsoever invented, to be a miserable calumny, a low malicious falsehood … a tale in every particular so unfounded.' Mrs Fitzherbert was greatly distressed by Fox's denial. The Prince summoned Lord Grey and told him Fox had gone 'too far'; a ceremony had taken place. Victorian legend has it that Henry Errington met Fox at the latter's club, Brooks's, and told him bluntly, 'You have been misinformed. I was present at the marriage,' but there is no evidence for this. Mrs Fitzherbert did not hide her resentment, and never forgave Fox, while Fox was in future wary of the Prince but did not formally break with him. Despite the kerfuffle, the Prince's debts were paid by Parliament, and Mrs Fitzherbert kept the Prince.

The marriage continued for nine years, with Mrs Fitzherbert accompanying the Prince to Brighton from London and back again – a round of dinners, cricket, picnics, races, dances, interior decoration – and generally putting up with boisterous Hanoverian behaviour, practical jokes, drunkenness and princely lies. She did her best to separate the Prince of Wales from his worst cronies and to maintain an atmosphere of domestic calm and peace, and to soothe tensions. Lady Hester Stanhope commented admiringly: 'Mrs Fitzherbert has a great deal of tact in concealing the Prince's faults.' Whig Society, the Catholic families, and the royal Dukes, especially the Dukes of Cumberland and Clarence, rallied round her. She was received privately by Queen Charlotte who thanked her for her good influence on the Prince.

A more serious threat to the Prince of Wales's marriage to Mrs Fitzherbert than the parliamentary row over the payment of his debts arose in 1788-89 with George III's first illness and the proposal that the Prince of Wales should be appointed Regent and exercise the King's powers. Could the Prince of Wales be Regent if he was married to a Roman Catholic? The crisis coincided with the centenary of the 1688 revolution and a wave of anti-Catholic feeling. Though the Regency Act was passed by Parliament, the King recovered, and the crisis passed.

Following the French Revolution, Mrs Fitzherbert, like Lady Jerningham, took the French *emigrés* under her wing. She opened her house in Brighton as a first staging post for priests, nuns and aristocrats fleeing from France. Her little Catholic oratory was soon packed to overflowing at mass. She opened a subscription to raise money for the English Benedictine nuns from Flanders who arrived at Shoreham on the Sussex coast and were put up at the *Ship Inn* in Brighton under Mrs Fitzherbert's and the Prince's protection, before being found a more permanent home in Warwickshire. Some of the refugees were old friends such as Catherine Dillon, a niece of Lady Jerningham's. Some of the refugees had dramatic escapes. The beautiful young Duchesse de Noailles turned up on Brighton beach disguised as a cabin boy in August 1792 and was taken into Mrs Fitzherbert's house. They rode out together on a daily basis, and attended cricket matches, while the Prince paid great attention to the duchess, with the 'humanity and gallantry which so invariably distinguished him.' In this sort of public relief work Mrs Fitzherbert was much assisted by her secretary-companion, or lady in waiting, Isabella Piggot, a woman of forthright 'even eccentric mien', who made a future career staying in country houses and amusing the company with royal gossip. 'Everybody was delighted to have her.'

The early 1790s in Brighton, looking after the French, provided Mrs Fitzherbert with the perfect outlet, using her social influence to the benefit of her unfortunate co-religionists from across the Channel. Unbeknown to her, however, the King, who had never recognised the relationship, was already making arrangements for the Prince of Wales's future which would destroy her marriage. By 1794 the Prince's debts, swelled by the constant remodelling and redecoration of Carlton House and Brighton Pavilion, had again climbed to the dizzy sum of £375,000. This time the King was only prepared to authorise their payment on condition that the Prince settled down and married a suitable Protestant German princess. The Queen sent Lady Jersey, a grandmotherly vamp, to the Prince to detach him from Mrs Fitzherbert prior to the German match, a task in which Lady Jersey more than fulfilled her potential, remaining the Prince's mistress for several years.

In the summer of 1794 Mrs Fitzherbert rented Marble Hill at Twickenham where she entertained on her usual generous scale. On the morning of 23 June she received an amiable note from the Prince addressed to 'My dearest love' saying that he was coming up to Town and Windsor from Brighton. That evening, while she dined with the Duke of Clarence, a note was handed to her at table. It was from the Prince and said that he never intended to see her again. She went home immediately, where she endorsed the first royal missive: 'This letter I received the morning of the day the Prince sent me word he would never enter my house,' and added 'Lady Jersey.' The break was the culmination of years of misunderstanding and quarrels for she had a quick temper and regal manner while he was often jealous of her social flirting.

The Prince married his cousin Princess Caroline of Brunswick by proxy in Germany in December 1794 and at the Chapel Royal St James's on 8 April 1795 in a haze of brandy. To Mrs Fitzherbert, after nine years of the Prince's moods, lies and hysterics, life as a widow may have seemed rather attractive. Whatever the Prince's faults, he was never mean with money (and he immediately regretted the 'misunderstanding' with Mrs Fitzherbert, telling his brother, the Duke of Clarence: 'She is the only woman I shall ever love.') and he continued to pay her £3,000 a year. She sold her house in Pall Mall and bought a smaller one, No 6 Tilney Street, off Park Lane in Mayfair, which remained her home for another forty years. There the Duke of Wellington, after her death, burnt most of her private papers in the drawing room grate, consigning unknowable mysteries to the flames.

The Prince's legal marriage was not a success, and he soon pined for Mrs Fitzherbert's return. Many members of the Royal Family also supported a reconciliation. After 12 months, and the birth of a daughter and heir, Princess Charlotte, the Prince of Wales separated from Princess Caroline. Mrs Fitzherbert understood that the Prince had been forced into an unhappy legal marriage by his father, and gave him the benefit of the doubt. She took advice from a Catholic priest (Fr Nassau at the Assumption, Warwick Street – the Portuguese Chapel) as to her status. He raised the matter with the Pope and received a positive reply that in the eyes of Rome the marriage was valid. Armed with this advice Mrs Fitzherbert returned to the Prince. Their rapprochement caused astonishment. Lady Jerningham wrote, 'The affairs of Mrs Fitzherbert and the Prince become very incomprehensible. It is a fact that he meets her whenever he can and a conversation ensues which takes them out of the company … I comprehend it no longer for I had thought Mrs Fitzherbert a woman of principle.' She was now forty-one. Years later she told Lord Stourton that she did not regret her reconciliation with the Prince. She thanked God she had the courage to do so. The next eight years were, she said, the happiest of her connection with the Prince. They lived as brother and sister, with separate social lives and separate houses.

She was now quite plump, delicious nine-course dinners prepared by the Prince's French chefs having taken their toll. He was more and more outrageous: drunker and drunker (cherry brandy was his favourite tipple) and the stories more and more fantastical. She loved her wicked, amusing, mercurial prince. She kept Tilney Street, but built a new house in Brighton in 1801 in the Egyptian style designed by William Porden, the architect of the Prince's new stables (in the Saracenic mode) at the Pavilion. The ultra-fashionable choice of Egyptian (following Napoleon's victories in Egypt and Nelson's Battle of the Nile) shows the impact of the Prince's advanced architectural tastes. On a future, less happy occasion, she referred to Porden as '*his* architect'. The house blew down in a storm, a strange augury. After 1807 the Prince and Mrs Fitzherbert gradually drifted apart. By 1811 all was over, and they never met again. The Prince became Regent, after the King went mad again in 1810, deserted the Whigs for the Tories, turned anti-Catholic and adopted Lady Hertford for his mistress. 'He has taken it into his head to fall desperately in love with Lady Hertford … without exception the most forbidding, haughty, unpleasant-looking woman I ever saw.' But the Prince and Lord Hertford shared the same taste in French furniture and the Hertfords were the legal guardians of little Mary, or Minnie, Seymour, one of Mrs Fitzherbert's two adopted daughters. Minnie Seymour was the orphan daughter of Hugh Seymour, a former courtier at Carlton House, whom Mrs Fitzherbert had taken into her house in 1801. The child was brought up in remarkably domestic circumstances, as their pseudo-daughter, by Mrs Fitzherbert and the Prince. The latter himself supported the application by Mrs Fitzherbert in the House of Lords to keep Minnie when the Hertfords objected on the grounds that Mrs Fitzherbert was a Catholic.

The final break was brought about by a calculated snub by the Prince Regent after his elevation to the Regency. In June 1811 he gave a gala dinner at Carlton House, with all his glistening new gold plate, to celebrate the Regency. The guests included King Louis XVIII of France (in exile). Mrs Fitzherbert had always sat at the head of the Prince's table as his wife. On this French royal occasion the Prince informed her that the guests would have to sit according to rank. She had the last word: 'I can never submit to appear in your house in any place or situation but in that where you yourself placed me many years ago.' The Prince, as always, was generous with money. He paid for a new house (also by Porden, this time in the French style) on the Steyne at Brighton, raised her allowance from £3,000 to £6,000 a year, and sent her a beautiful pearl necklace which remains in the family. When he became king in 1820 he put up her income to £10,000 p.a. which was the income he had originally promised when he married her but had hitherto been prevented from paying by his chaotic finances.

Mrs Fitzherbert embarked once more on serene widowhood, one of the leading Catholic dowagers of London. She became more devout as she grew older. On the return of the Bourbons, she re-visited Paris in 1815 and was received by Louis XVIII at the Tuilleries. In the same year she added the name of Marianne Smythe to her visiting card – introducing the girl as her niece. She was the illegitimate daughter of Mrs Fitzherbert's favourite brother John Smythe who had died in 1813. It was rumoured, without foundation, that she, too, was a daughter of Mrs Fitzherbert by George IV, like Minnie Seymour (the orphaned daughter of Hugh Seymour) who had been 'adopted' and brought up by Mrs Fitzherbert. The Anglican Minnie married George Dawson Damer, younger son of the Earl of Portarlington and a 'penniless cavalry officer' who soon became one of Mrs Fitzherbert's *confidantes*. Colonel Dawson Damer and Minnie moved into Tilney Street with Mrs Fitzherbert and lived with her in her old age. In her 70s Mrs Fitzherbert was surrounded by adoring young – nieces,

81 Drawing by Henry Bunch of Marianne
Smythe at Brighton, 1814. Marianne was the
niece and adopted daughter of Mrs Fitzherbert.
She married the Hon. Edward Jerningham, the
younger son of the 8th Lord Stafford.

81 Marianne (Smythe) Jerningham, 1842.
Portrait by G.M. Brightly.

godchildren, friends – who called her 'Aunt Fitz', and ancient servants, whom she
called 'The Treasures', and who had been with her for years.

Prince Puckler Müskau, a wife-hunting German adventurer and connoisseur of
landscape gardening, who attended a whist party given by Mrs Fitzherbert at Brighton
in February 1827, left a vivid pen portrait of her. 'I spent this evening at Mrs Fitzherbert's,
a very dignified and delightful woman, formerly as it is affirmed, married to the King.
She is now without influence in that region, but still universally beloved and respected
– 'd'un excellent ton et sans pretention' She lived over six years longer than George IV who
died in 1830. When she heard the King was very ill, she sent him a last letter which
he read and put under his pillow. He was buried with her miniature in a locket which
he had always worn. Mrs Fitzherbert died on Easter Monday 1837 at Brighton where
she was buried. The effigy on her tomb has three wedding rings on her finger.

Mrs Fitzherbert's Catholic niece Marianne Smythe, who had lived with her since
the age of six, married the Hon Edward Stafford-Jerningham, second son of George,
8th Lord Stafford, and an officer in the 6th Dragoon Guards, in June 1828. Mrs
Fitzherbert liked him from the start and thought him 'very amiable, good-looking and
gentlemanlike'. Edward and Marianne's son succeeded as 10th Lord Stafford in 1884.
He was declared insane, however, and on his death in 1892 their younger son Fitzherbert
Stafford-Jerningham (so-called after Mrs Fitzherbert) succeeded as 11th (and last
Jerningham) Lord Stafford. Marianne and Edward's daughter Emily Charlotte (born 31

83 Mrs Fitzherbert. Portrait by Richard Cosway.

March 1835) married in 1858 Basil Thomas Fitzherbert. After her brothers' deaths, the Stafford barony was inherited by Emily's son Francis Edward Fitzherbert-Stafford. That brought the Stafford title to the family of Mrs Fitzherbert's former husband Thomas Fitzherbert.

Mrs Fitzherbert in later life was a rich woman in her own right. Her jointure from her two early marriages amounted to £8,000 a year, and in addition after 1820 she received £10,000 a year from George IV (continued after his death by William IV and Queen Victoria out of the Civil List). Over the years she had also received many presents from the Prince. She was shrewd with her money, invested well, and had always been good with property, selling her various houses for a profit. She was thus in a position to be very generous to both her adopted daughters. On her death they became her joint heiresses and inherited her fortune half each. When Marianne married Edward Jerningham, Mrs Fitzherbert had also given them £20,000. She bequeathed her presents from George IV to her adopted daughters and it is as a result of this that her portrait by Richard Cosway, miniatures, magnificent pearl necklace, work box and gold and blue enamelled snuff box given to her by the King, descended to the Lords Stafford.

POSTSCRIPT

The Fitzherberts

❧ · ❧

T HE FITZHERBERTS of Swynnerton in Staffordshire, like the Jerninghams, were a medieval knightly family who had remained Catholic after the 16th-century reformation, living quietly on their Midlands estates and inter-marrying with other Catholic recusant dynasties. Like their maternal ancestors and previous holders of the title they could trace their line back almost to the Norman Conquest in the male line. William Fitzherbert of Norbury in Derbyshire had a grant of that manor from the Prior of Tutbury in 112⁵ The charter, attested by, among others, Robert de Ferrers, Earl of Derby, the Bishop of Lichfield and the Abbot of Burton, is still in the possession of Lord Stafford.

The Fitzherberts held Norbury down to the late 19th century and produced some notable figures in the Middle Ages and 16th century, such as Sir Anthony Fitzherbert of Norbury, an eminent lawyer, Justice of the Common Pleas under Henry VIII and author of several legal works such as *La Grande Abridgement.* His fourth son, William of Somersall in Staffordshire, married Elizabeth, co-heiress of Humphry Swynnerton of Swynnerton in Staffordshire, bringing that estate to the Fitzherberts. Their son Thomas Fitzherbert of Swynnerton who lived to the great age of 88 (dying during the Civil War in 1640), was a strong Catholic and wrote many devotional works. He established the future pattern of the family as Catholic squires living at Swynnerton. His great-grandson, Basil, inherited the old medieval manor house at Norbury on the extinction of the senior line at the beginning of the 18th century. Basil's great-great-grandson in turn was Thomas, the husband of Maria Smythe, *the* Mrs Fitzherbert. The medieval house at Swynnerton, 'Mr Fitzherbert's castle', was destroyed in the Civil War by order of the parliamentary committee at Stafford on 29 February 1643/4 at the same time as Stafford Castle. Subsequently, a handsome new house of ashlar stone was built on a different, more elevated site, for Thomas Fitzherbert from 1725-9 to the design of Francis Smith of Warwick, and the surrounding park was landscaped

84 Francis Fitzherbert, 12th Lord Stafford.
Portrait by J. Halliday.

85 Admiral Edward Fitzherbert, 13th Lord
Stafford. Portrait by Richard Marientreau.

later in the 18th century in the manner of 'Capability' Brown. In about 1810 James
Trubshaw (a local Staffordshire architect) remodelled the interior of the house for
Thomas Fitzherbert in the fashionable Regency style. These elegant rooms (handsomely
restored and redecorated by the present Lord Stafford and his wife) form the setting
both for the Fitzherbert family portraits and heirlooms and also those inherited from
the Jerninghams of Costessey with the Stafford barony and Stafford Castle.

Francis Edward Fitzherbert of Swynnerton, who succeeded his maternal uncle as
12th Lord Stafford in 1913, inherited some of the remaining contents of Costessey
including family portraits, furniture and plate (though much had been sold at Christie's
in 1885), but not Costessey Hall itself nor the 3,000-acre Norfolk estate which passed
with the baronetcy to William Jerningham, the last male member of his family, which

86 Swynnerton Hall, Staffordshire.

has been sold. Costessey Hall itself was demolished *c.*1925, a notable 20th-century loss among country houses. Francis Edward was a career soldier and had fought in the South African War, winning the D.S.O. On his death in 1932, he was succeeded by his younger brother, Edward, who was an admiral and had served in the navy all over the world during the zenith of Victorian sea power, and with distinction in the First World War as Captain of the *Colossus* in the Grand Fleet, and Director of Torpedoes. He was unmarried, and on his death in 1941 the barony was inherited by his nephew Basil, the father of Francis, the 15th and present Lord Stafford, who has commissioned this short history of the family.

Pedigree of Early Staffords & Dukes of Buckingham

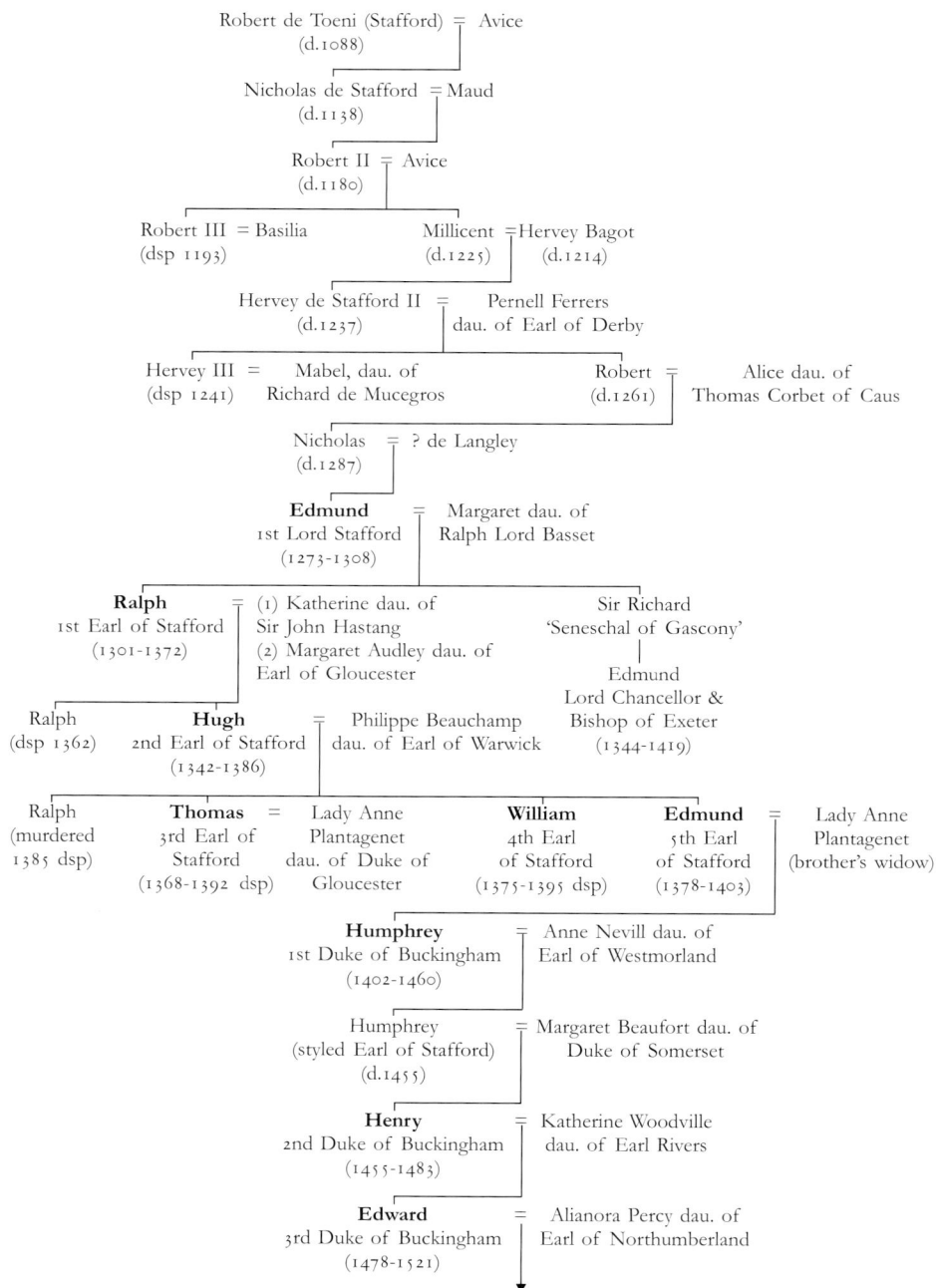

Robert de Toeni (Stafford) = Avice
(d.1088)

Nicholas de Stafford = Maud
(d.1138)

Robert II = Avice
(d.1180)

Robert III = Basilia   Millicent = Hervey Bagot
(dsp 1193)   (d.1225)   (d.1214)

Hervey de Stafford II = Pernell Ferrers
(d.1237)   dau. of Earl of Derby

Hervey III = Mabel, dau. of   Robert = Alice dau. of
(dsp 1241)   Richard de Mucegros   (d.1261)   Thomas Corbet of Caus

Nicholas = ? de Langley
(d.1287)

Edmund = Margaret dau. of
1st Lord Stafford   Ralph Lord Basset
(1273-1308)

Ralph = (1) Katherine dau. of   Sir Richard
1st Earl of Stafford   Sir John Hastang   'Seneschal of Gascony'
(1301-1372)   (2) Margaret Audley dau. of
     Earl of Gloucester   Edmund
                               Lord Chancellor &
Ralph   **Hugh** = Philippe Beauchamp   Bishop of Exeter
(dsp 1362)   2nd Earl of Stafford   dau. of Earl of Warwick   (1344-1419)
        (1342-1386)

Ralph   **Thomas** = Lady Anne   **William**   **Edmund** = Lady Anne
(murdered   3rd Earl of   Plantagenet   4th Earl   5th Earl   Plantagenet
1385 dsp)   Stafford   dau. of Duke of   of Stafford   of Stafford   (brother's widow)
        (1368-1392 dsp)   Gloucester   (1375-1395 dsp)   (1378-1403)

Humphrey = Anne Nevill dau. of
1st Duke of Buckingham   Earl of Westmorland
(1402-1460)

Humphrey = Margaret Beaufort dau. of
(styled Earl of Stafford)   Duke of Somerset
(d.1455)

Henry = Katherine Woodville
2nd Duke of Buckingham   dau. of Earl Rivers
(1455-1483)

Edward = Alianora Percy dau. of
3rd Duke of Buckingham   Earl of Northumberland
(1478-1521)

Pedigree of Stafford Howard

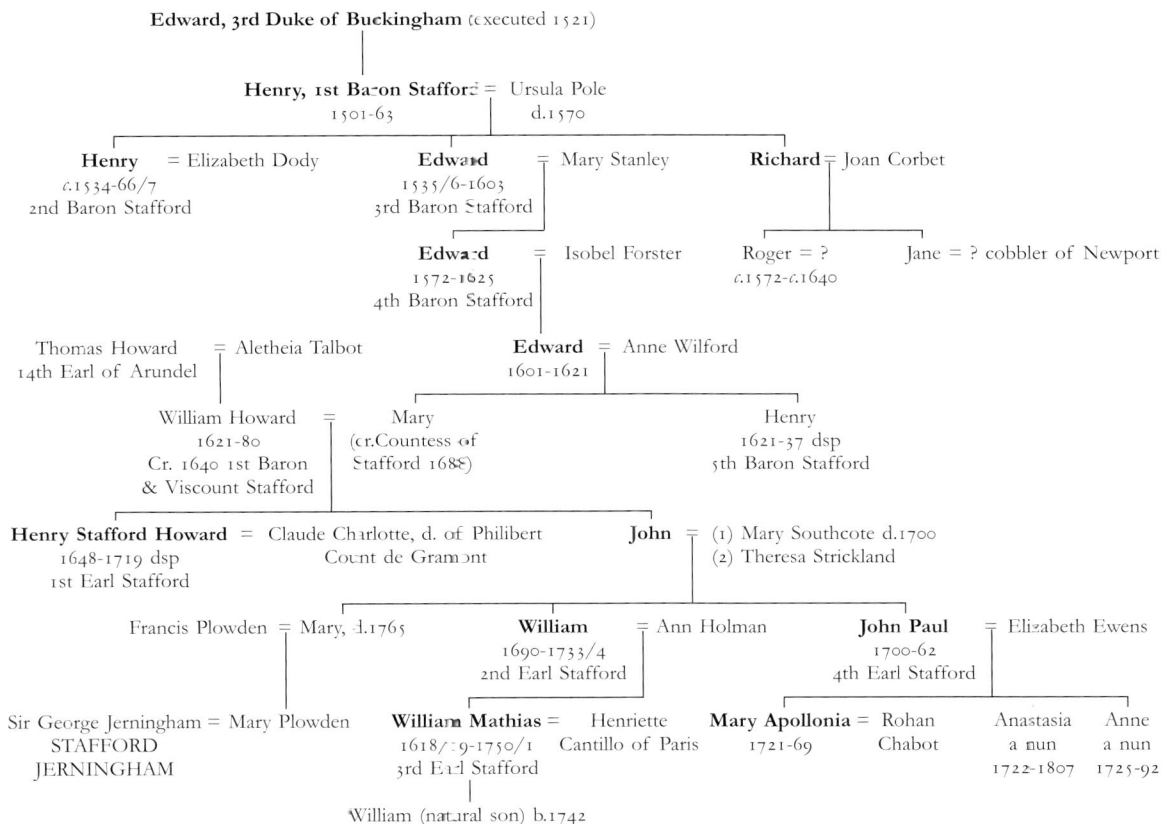

Edward, 3rd Duke of Buckingham (executed 1521)

Henry, 1st Baron Stafford = Ursula Pole
1501-63   d.1570

Henry = Elizabeth Dody   **Edward** = Mary Stanley   **Richard** = Joan Corbet
c.1534-66/7   1535/6-1603
2nd Baron Stafford   3rd Baron Stafford

Edward = Isobel Forster   Roger = ?   Jane = ? cobbler of Newport
1572-1625   c.1572-c.1640
4th Baron Stafford

Edward = Anne Wilford
1601-1621

Thomas Howard = Aletheia Talbot
14th Earl of Arundel

William Howard = Mary   Henry
1621-80   (cr.Countess of   1621-37 dsp
Cr. 1640 1st Baron   Stafford 1688)   5th Baron Stafford
& Viscount Stafford

Henry Stafford Howard = Claude Charlotte, d. of Philibert   **John** = (1) Mary Southcote d.1700
1648-1719 dsp   Count de Gramont   (2) Theresa Strickland
1st Earl Stafford

Francis Plowden = Mary, d.1765   **William** = Ann Holman   **John Paul** = Elizabeth Ewens
                   1690-1733/4   1700-62
                   2nd Earl Stafford   4th Earl Stafford

Sir George Jerningham = Mary Plowden   **William Mathias** = Henriette   **Mary Apollonia** = Rohan   Anastasia   Anne
STAFFORD   1618/19-1750/1   Cantillo of Paris   1721-69   Chabot   a nun   a nun
JERNINGHAM   3rd Earl Stafford   1722-1807   1725-92

William (natural son) b.1742

The Fitzherberts of Norbury

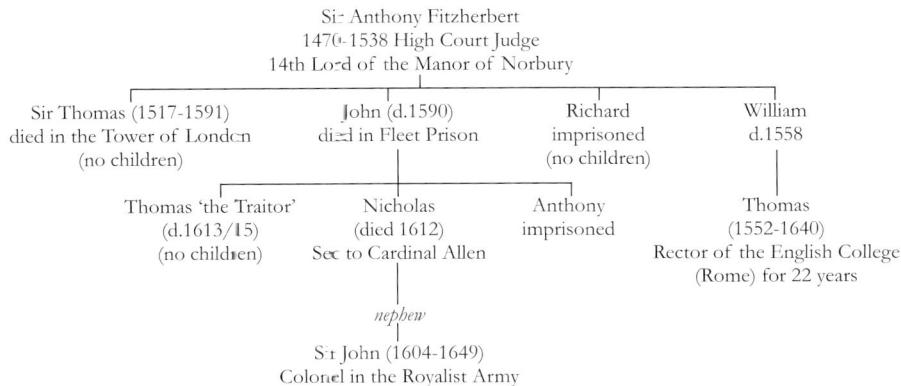

Sir Anthony Fitzherbert
1470-1538 High Court Judge
14th Lord of the Manor of Norbury

Sir Thomas (1517-1591)   John (d.1590)   Richard   William
died in the Tower of London   died in Fleet Prison   imprisoned   d.1558
(no children)   (no children)

Thomas 'the Traitor'   Nicholas   Anthony   Thomas
(d.1613/15)   (died 1612)   imprisoned   (1552-1640)
(no children)   Sec to Cardinal Allen   Rector of the English College
                                            (Rome) for 22 years

nephew

Sir John (1604-1649)
Colonel in the Royalist Army

Pedigree of Stafford Jerningham and Fitzherbert

Sir George Jerningham = Mary Plowden
1680-1774   d.1783

William   = Frances Dillon   Edward 'The Poet'   Charles 'Chevalier' d.1814
6th Bart.   d.1825
1736-1809

George William = (1) Frances Sulyard, d.1832   William Charles = (1) Anne Wright   Edward = Emily   Charlotte = Sir Richard
7th Bart.   (2) Elizabeth Caton   1772-1820   (2) Ann Moore   1774-1822 Middleton   d.1845   Bedingfield
8th Baron
1771-1851

Frederick = Georgina Howe   Charles = Emma Wynn
1813-70   d.1894   1805-54   d.1888

Adolphus = Matilda Riley   Sir Hubert Edward Henry = Annie Liddall
1842-1904   1842-1914 dsp

Henry Valentine = (1) Julia Howard   Edward = Marianne Smythe   William Henry
8th Bart.   (2) Emma Gerard   1804-1849 (adopted dau. of   11th Bart.
9th Baron   Mrs Fitzherbert)   1867-1935 dsp
1802-84 dsp   c.1859

Augustus   **Fitzherbert Edward**   Emily (Charlotte) = Basil Thomas Fitzherbert
9th Bart.   10th Bart.   1835-81   1836-1919
10th Baron   11th Baron
1830-92 dsp   dsp 1913

Francis Edward   = Dorothy Worthington   **Edward**   Thomas
12th Baron Stafford   d.1958   13th Baron Stafford   1869-1937
1859-1932   1864-1941 dsp

Basil   = Morag Campbell
14th Baron Stafford
1926-86

Francis   = Katherine Codrington
15th Baron Stafford
1954-

Benjamin   Toby   Teresa   Camilla Rose Jane
1983   1985   1987   1989

Notes

I The Origins of the Stafford Family & Stafford Castle pp.1-6

1 For an alternative history of Stafford Castle, see D. M. Palliser, 'The Castles at Stafford', *Stafford Historical and Civic Society* (1971-3), 1-17.

2 *V.C.H. Staffordshire*, V, 82-84; J. Darlington, ed., *Stafford Castle: Survey, excavation and research 1978-1998* (Stafford Borough Council, 2001), T. J. de Mazzhingi, 'History of Castle Church,' *Staff. Hist Coll.* VII (II) (1887), 1-152.

3 *Stafford Castle: A Brief History* (Stafford Borough Council, 1988, reprinted 2001); C. Hill, *Stafford Castle: interim reports* (Stafford Borough Council) 1980-1982.

4 Domesday Book vol. I ff 248b, 242b, 368b, 158, 176b, 225, 376b-377b, vol ii f445b; Mazzhingi, *op. cit.*, 55-57.

5 Sir William Dugdale, *Monasticon Anglicanum* (Revised edition 1718), 136, 269.

6 *Stafford Castle: a brief history, op. cit.*; William Salt Library: Eyton, *Historical Collections Staffs.*, II part 1, 211, 260, 193.

7 *Stafford Castle, Interim Reports, op. cit.*

8 Carole Rawcliffe, *The Staffords, Earls of Stafford and Dukes of Buckingham 1394-1521* (1978); *Complete Peerage* XII/1, 173.

II Earls and Bishops pp.7-18

1 *Complete Peerage* XII/1, 174.

2 Carole Rawcliffe, *The Staffords, Earls of Stafford and Dukes of Buckingham 1394-1521* (Cambridge University Press, 1978) 9-10.

3 Froissart's *Chronicles* IV, 214, 274, 286; V, 216.

4 Staffordshire Record Office, D(W) 1721/1/1; 1721/1/II.

5 *V.C.H., op. cit.*, 84.

6 Froissart, *op. cit.*, II, 305.

7 There is a little portrait of Ralph holding a shield of the Stafford arms among the mourners in the borders of the sumptuous brass to Hugh Hastings in Elsing church, Norfolk.

8 *D.N.B.*

9 Harold Cole, 'Humphrey Stafford First Duke of Buckingham,' (London University MA Thesis 1945) 269 Appendix C.

10 William Stubbs, *Constitutional History* (1900) III.

11 *Complete Peerage*, XII/1, 179 f.n. i

12 Sir William Dugdale, *Baronage of England*, III (1676).

13 Rawcliffe *op. cit.*, 10-11.

14 Rawcliffe *op. cit.*, 16-17.

III **The Dukes of Buckingham** pp.19-34

1 Rawcliffe, *op. cit.*, 18-19.
2 Harold Cole, 'Humphrey Stafford First Duke of Buckingham 1402-1460', London University MA Thesis 1945, pp.24-5, 205-7.
3 Dugdale, *Baronage, op. cit.*, 165.
4 Cole, *op. cit.*, 69-74.
5 *Complete Peerage.*
6 Stevenson, *Wars of England in France* II, 619.
7 Stevenson, *Wars of England in France*, I, 101-38.
8 Richard Turpyn, *Chronicle of Calais*, Henry VI Anno 21-Anno 29 (Camden Society, 1861).
9 Rot Parl V, 206.
10 Calendar of the Patent Rolls (1909), Henry VI, V, 473.
11 Cole, *op. cit.*, 42.
12 *Historical Manuscripts Commission* X Report iv, 55, Receivers Account for Dover.
13 Cole, *op. cit.*, 81-95; Dugdale, *Monasticon, op. cit.*, II, 165.
14 See *Paston Letters* I, 61.
15 *Paston Letters,* I, 355-7.
16 *Paston Letters*, I, 407-9.
17 Cole, *op. cit.*, 195-207.
18 K.B. McFarlane, *The Nobility of Later Medieval England* (O.U.P. 1973), 187-212.
19 *Complete Peerage*, II, Appendix D, 605.
20 Rawcliffe, *op. cit.*, 121-6.

IV **The Tragedy of the Third Duke** pp.35-48

1 This was the paper estimate in his estate valors, though, in effect, the difficulties of revenue collection meant he never received the full income and died seriously in debt.
2 B.J. Harris, *Edward Stafford 3rd Duke of Buckingham* (Stafford University Press, 1986), 29-31.
3 Harris, *op. cit.*, 42-3.
4 Rawcliffe, *op. cit.*
5 *V.C.H., op. cit.*, 85.
6 Harris, *op. cit.*, 77.
7 Harris, *op. cit.*, 134.
8 J.N. Langston, 'The Staffords of Thornbury Castle', *Bristol & Gloucester Archaeological Society*, 72 (1953), 83.
9 See David Skinner, 'Nicholas Ludford … with a study of the Collegiate Chapel of the Holy Trinity, Arundel', D. Phil. Thesis, Oxford, 1997.
10 Harris, *op. cit.*, 91.
11 Staffordshire Record Office, Household Accounts, 13 November 1507 D1721/1/5, f6.
12 Staffordshire Record Office, D1721/1/5 ff 46, 58, 59.
13 J. Gage, ed., 'Extracts from the Household Book of Edward Duke of Buckingham 1508-9,' *Archaeologia,* xxv (1834), 311.
14 Staffordshire Record Office, D641/1/3/10.
15 Rawcliffe, *op. cit.*, 2; the surviving nucleus of these papers is now in the Staffordshire Record Office.
16 Harris, *op. cit.*, 36
17 Harris, *op. cit.*, 162.
18 Langston, *op. cit.*, 83-4.
19 Rawcliffe, *op. cit.*, 166-8.
20 Rawcliffe, *op. cit.*, 170-3.
21 M Levine, *The Fall of the Duke of Buckingham* (Louisiana, 1972).

V **From Dukes to Shoemakers** pp.49-66

1 Three manors worth £78 p.a. were given to Richard Jerningham, ancestor of the family which inherited the Stafford barony in the 19th century.
2 *Complete Peerage* XII/1, 183.

3 Rawcliffe, *op. cit.*, 2; Staffordshire Record Office DW1721/1/1 & 2.

4 M.A.E. Wood Green, *Letters of Royal and Illustrious Ladies of Great Britain,* (1846) II, 189.

5 Charles Henry Cooper, *Athenae Cantabrigenses* (Cambridge, 1858) I, 216.

6 *Complete Peerage* XII/1, 183.

7 *V.C.H., op. cit.*, 85.

8 Mary Hervey, *Life of Thomas Earl of Arundel* (1921), 207.

9 Staffordshire Record Office, D946/2; D641/2II/1-3.

10 Langston, *op. cit.*, 83-4.

11 Camden Society, II, 138, 'Wriothesley's Chronicle'.

12 Hatfield Mss ii, 224, Lord Burghley.

13 *Complete Peerage*, IV, sub Derby, Note.

14 Conyers Read, 'The fame of Sir Edward Stafford', *American Historical Review* XX (1915), 292-315; J. E. Neale, 'The fame of Sir Edward Stafford,' *English Historical Review* XLIV (1929) 203-20; Conyers Read, 'The fame of Sir Edward Stafford, *American Historical Review* XXV (1915) 560-6.

15 Sir Bernard Burke, *Noble Families* (18).

16 *Complete Peerage* XII/1, 188-92.

17 J.M. Robinson, *The Dukes of Norfolk* (O.U.P. 1982); Henry Howard, *Memorials of the Howard Family* (1834).

18 He died a Catholic at Padua in 1646 where he received the Last Sacraments from a Jesuit priest. *Ex info* Prof Edward Chaney.

19 Gerald Brennan and Edward Statham, *The House of Howard* (1907) II, 586.

20 Mary Hervey, *Thomas Howard Earl of Arundel* (Cambridge University Press, 1921); David Howard, *Lord Arundel & His Circle* (1985).

21 Mary Hervey, *op. cit.*, 523.

22 P.R.O. C54/3017, No. 12: Indenture of Sale, 1633; *Ex info* Dr Elizabeth Chew.

23 *Stafford Catle*, Third Interim Report, 1981, 11.

24 Colleen Marie Seguin, 'Addicted Unto Piety: Catholic Women in England 1590-1690', Dissertation, Duke University (1997).

25 *Stafford's Memoires: Or a Brief and Impartial Account of the Birth and Quality, Imprisonment, Tryal, Principles, Declaration, Comportment, Devotion, Last Speech and Final End of William, late Viscount Stafford ...* (1681).

26 Elizabeth Chew, 'Art Collecting & Patronage in Seventeenth Century England,' PhD Thesis, University of North Carolina (1999).

VI **Viscount Stafford and the Earls of Stafford** pp.67-78

1 P.R.O.: Court of Delegates Possesses VII No 14, 881; M.A.E. Green, ed., *Calendar of the Proceedings of the Committee for the Advance of Money 1642-56.*

2 P.R.O.: SP23/62/677; SP19/143/26 & 29; Elizabeth Chew, 'Art Collecting & Patronage in Seventeenth Century England,' PhD Thesis, University of North Carolina (1999).

3 *V.C.H. Shropshire*, I, 404; XI, Telford (1985), 311.

4 P.R.O. Delegates Processes, VII, No. 14.

5 Mary Coe, *Sir William Howard, Viscount Stafford* (1927) 94; Arundel Castle MSS G2/13; Transcripts of all papers in the P.R.O. relating to William, Viscount Stafford.

6 J.M. Robinson, *The Dukes of Norfolk, op. cit.*; Gerald Brennan and Edward Statham, *The House of Howard* (1907) II, 586-590.

7 Lords Arundell of Wardour, Bellasis and Petre and the Earl of Powis.

8 *Stafford's Memoires, op. cit.*

9 William Braye, ed., *Diary of John Evelyn* (1818) I, 496; Brennan and Statham, *op. cit.*, 590.

10 Viscount Stafford prepared eight different drafts of his last speech.

11 *Stafford's Memoires, op. cit.*

12 A.M. Crino, *Fatti' Figure del Seicento* (Florence, 1957), 134.

13 *The Speech of Wil. Howard Lord Viscount Stafford ... on Wednesday December 29 1680.* (Printed for J. Clarke, Smithfield.)

14 *A Catalogue of the Pictures, Prints, Drawings etc being part of the old Arundel Collection and belonging to the Late Earl of Stafford* (1720).

15 *Walpole Society* 26 (1937-8) 26-7; 'Vertue Notebooks' V.

16 Arundel Castle, George Vertue 'Howard Memorials' (MS 1737); A.C. MSS in 77.

17 Arundel Castle MSS, T50, Will of William 2nd Earl Stafford.

VII **The Jerninghams** pp.79-96

1 Quoted in *Viscount Stafford, op. cit.*, 222.

2 An accurate early pedigree of the family can be found in the Revd Francis Blomefield, *History of Norfolk* (1739) Vol I, 658.

3 *Gents. Mag.*, LXXVI pt ii.

4 Egerton Castle, ed., *Jerningham Letters 1780-1843* (1896) 2 vols, I, 26 March 1802. The original correspondence is in the Staffordshire Record Office, D641/3P/3/128-148.

5 *Jerningham Letters*, I, *op. cit.*, 15 October 1803.

6 *Jerningham Letters*, I, *op. cit.*, 26 March 1802.

7 *Jerningham Letters*, *op. cit.*

8 Major Trappes Lomax, 'Diary of Edward Jerningham' (MS).

9 Lewis Bettany, *Edward Jerningham and His Friends* (New York, 1919), 3-5.

10 *Jerningham Letters*, *op. cit.*, I.

11 *Jerningham Letters*, *op. cit.* II.

12 Bethany, *op. cit.*

13 *Jerningham Letters*, *op. cit.*, 4 April 1807.

14 *Jerningham Letters*, I, *op. cit.*, 15 August 1785.

15 *Jerningham Letters*, *op. cit.*, 1784; Mark Bence-Jones, *The Catholic Families* (1992).

16 *Jerningham Letters*, I, *op. cit.*, 24 October 1784.

17 *Jerningham Letters*, 6 March 1786.

18 *Jerningham Letters*, 15 September 1785.

19 V.C.H. *Shropshire* XI (1985) Telford.

20 Charlotte's Parisian schooling cost £200 p.a. – a very substantial sum in the 18th century.

21 *Jermingham Letters*, I, *op. cit.*, 1792.

22 *Jerningham Letters*, I, *op. cit.*, 26 March 1802; 2 September 1802.

23 *Jerningham Letters*, I, *op. cit.*, May 1800.

24 *Jerningham Letters* I, *op. cit.*, 1797; Charlotte Bedingfeld to Lady Jerningham.

25 It is a 'fess dancettee the upper points terminating in fleur de lys'.

26 Staffordshire Record Office, D641/3/P/4/14/5.

27 Staffordshire Record Office, D641/3.

28 Bence Jones, *Catholic Families, op. cit.*, 114, 125.

VIII **The Revival of the Stafford Peerage** pp.97-110

1 *Jerningham Letters*, I *op. cit.*, 22 May 1807.

2 Staffordshire Record Office, D641/3/N/1/1/1/1-5; M/1/2/1-16; D641/M/1/ 3/1-24.

3 Clive Wainright, *The Romantic Interior* (1989), 284.

4 *Victorian Society Annual* (1997), 26-7; Harry Gunton, 'Costessey Brickworks', *Trans. Newcomen Soc.* (1968) XL, 165-8.

5 Staffordshire Record Office, D641/3/P/3/23, D641/13/a/1-3, 15-16, 19-21, 23-30; Wainright, *op. cit.*, 282-4.

6 T.B. Norgate, *History of Costessey* (1972).

7 Revd R.C. Husenbeth, *Discourse Pronounced at the Funeral of Frances Xavaria, Baroness Stafford,* 27 November 1832.

8 H.E. Jerningham, *Reminiscences of an Attaché* (1886).

9 Staffordshire Record Office, D641/3/N/22/1-3; Journals of G.S.S. Jerningham.

10 *Ibid.*, D641/3/N/24/1.

11 *Ibid.*, D641.

12 Arundel Castle MSS, MD 1702 – Costessey: Catalogue of Books & MSS Sold 28 July 1885.

13 Ian Anstruther, *The Knight and the Umbrella* (1963), 185.

Select Bibliography

❧ · ❧

MANUSCRIPTS

Arundel Castle MSS

Autograph letters 1617-1632: (no.293) Anne Stafford, 10 June 1631

Howard letters and papers 1636-1822: Elizabeth Mary Michael, Countess of Stafford to Miss Howard of Greystoke. 1769

Howard letters 1687-1735: two letters to Bernard Howard from Louisa Stafford, 1733, 1735/6

Staffordshire Maps TP274: Manor of Forebridge the property of Sir Wm. Jerningham, c.1775

G/4-46: Interim introduction to an account of the Swynnerton Hall MSS. Pt. I relating to the Stafford family prior to c.1575. 1 doc., 1969

G2/13, G2/14, G2/15: Henry, 1st Earl of Stafford (1648-1719) and William, 1st Baron and Viscount Stafford, 1612-80

AP 67: Parliamentary Bill for reversing the attainder of William, late Viscount Stafford, 1824

T50: Copy of will, 19 July 1733, and codicils, 21 July and 13 August 1733 (proved 28 February 1733/4 and 15 December 1736), of William, 2nd Earl of Stafford (1690-1733)

BN: Lord Stafford and Lady Ursula's Household Book, 1546

MD 489: Value of Lands, etc., of Edward, Duke of Buckingham, Mich. 1511-12. 1 roll

A 1655/7: Compoti for Manor of Stalbrook belonging to the Earl of Stafford, 1352-8

MD 1678: Compotus of John Bradley, receiver of Nicholas de Stafford et al., feoffees of Hugh, late Earl of Stafford, 1386-7

A 1411: Summary of rental of property and estates of Anne, Countess of Stafford, 1421

A 1245: Compotus of the receiver-general of the estates of Edward, Duke of Buckingham, 1497-8

A 1046: Compotus of the receiver-general of the estates of Edward, Duke of Buckingham, 1502-3

A 1252: Vouchers relating to estates of Henry, Lord Stafford, 1531-2

T 141: Draft Will, 20 February 1251, of Humphrey, Duke of Buckingham

MD 489: Valor of all castles etc. of Edward, Duke of Buckingham, Mich. 1511-12

A 1312: Receipts of payments by Henry, 1st Earl of Stafford and orders for payments made by Mary Howard (ss executrix) and Henry Charles Howard, 1714-21

A 125: Accounts of Henry Stafford Howard, 1st Earl of Stafford (1648-1719) and of his executor, Charles Howard, 1718-45

G3/79: Report on Earldoms of Buckingham, etc., cited in Lord Mowbray's supp. Case, 1904

G3/90-96: Memoranda etc. on other Earldoms etc.

MD 1920: Notice relating to Lord Stafford's Settled Estates 1909. (Fitzherbert 11th Lord Stafford)

MD 1702: Catalogue of books and MSS, the property of the late Lord Stafford of Costessy Hall, sold 28 July 1885

FC 612-617: Draft and copy deeds relating to family estates of, *inter al.*, Henry Valentine, 9th Baron Stafford, 1835-67

MD 2257: Correspondence and reports relating to Julia, Lady Stafford's Trust and to the Settled Estates of Fitzherbert, 11th Baron Stafford, 1879-1916

A 1883: Detailed rental of the lands of Edmund, Earl of Stafford, 1400-1

County Record Office, Stafford

D641/1: Records of the medieval Staffords, Earls of Stafford, and Dukes of Buckingham up to *c.*1560-80. There are very large numbers of records of estate administration, both financial and manorial together with some household records

D641/2: The Stafford-Howards, 1640-1762 but containing 16th- and early 17th-century documents assembled for legal/administrative purposes at a later date after 1640

D641/3: Stafford-Jerningham: in addition to family papers relating to the Jerningham family from the Middle Ages there are papers related to the period when the Stafford-Jerninghams owned the Stafford family estates

D641/3/G: Architectural Plans and Drawings for the reconstruction of Costessy

D641/3/M: Stafford Peerage Case

D641/3/Pl: Personal finance and accounts

D641/3/P3: Personal correspondence

D641/5: Fitzherbert. This family succeeded to the barony in 1913. There are no documents relating to the Stafford family estates among their records

Public Record Office

PRO/SP19/143/26: Testimony of a Nicholas Cheltenham that Tart Hall belonged to the Countess as part of her jointure. Tart Hall accounts

PRO/SP19/143/29: Accounts from 1650 showing payments for the upkeep of Tart Hall

PRO/SP23/11/67: This shows that Lady Arundel was in control of property all around Gowborough and Graystock, as it was being seized and sequestered

PRO/SP/23/36/13: William Crowne testifies before the committee in 1650 that 'he several times waited upon the Countess of Arundel to Somerset House when the Queen was there at Mass, and that she hath gone in and stayed there until the service was done And that he hath heard her servants say that she went to Mass in a long gallery at Arundel House and severall tyumes to Signor Cons house the Popes nuncio.' [Henrietta Maria had a spectacular Catholic Chapel in Somerset House, and the papal agent George Con maintained a well-attended chapel in his house in Long Acre.]

PRO/SP23/62/677: Suggestion that Lady Arundel was planning to return to England in 1652, as she sends an order to prepare Tart Hall for her use

PRO/C54/3017, No. 12: Indenture of Sale, 1633
PRO Court of Delegates Processes VII, No. 14, 881
PRO SP23/62/677; SP19/43/26 and 29
PRO Delegates Processes, VII, No. 14

Miscellaneous MSS

Major Trappes Lomax, 'Diary of Edward Jerningham' (MS)
Jones, Michael, 'History of the Fitzherbert Family,' 2 vols., MS (Early 19th century)
Salt Library. D 1850. (Stafford), The Revd J.B. Smith, Antiquaries Notes

PRINTED WORKS

Anstruther, Ian, *The Knight and the Umbrella* (1963)
Barker, Phillip and Barker, Peter, *The archaeological and social potential of Stafford Castle* (West Mercian Archaeological Consultants, 1978)
Bence-Jones, Mark, *The Catholic Families* (Constable, 1992)
Bettany, Lewis, *Edward Jerringham and His Friends* (New York, 1919), 3-5
Blomefield, Revd Francis, *History of Norfolk* (1739) vol. I. (An accurate early pedigree of the family)
Braye, William (Ed.), *Memoirs of John Evelyn* (London, 1818) I
Brennan, Gerald and Statham, Edward, *The House of Howard* (1907) II
Burke, Sir Bernard, *Noble Families* (1856)
Calendar of the Patent Rolls (1909). Henry VI, V, 473
Chew, Elizabeth, 'Art Collecting and Patronage in Seventeenth Century England' (PhD Thesis, University of North Carolina, 1999)
Coe, Mary, *Sir William Howard, Viscount Stafford* (1927)
Cole, Harold, 'Humphrey Stafford First Duke of Buckingham 1402-1460; an estimate of the significance of his political career', (London University MA Thesis, 1945)
The Complete Peerage of England Scotland Ireland Great Britain and the United Kingdom, vol. 5 (XI-XII/1; reprinted 2000)
Cooper, Charles Henry, *Athenae Cantabrigenses* (Cambridge, 1858) I, 216
Crino, A. M., *Fatti' Figure del Seicento* (Florence, 1957)
Darlington, John (Ed.), *Stafford Castle: Survey, excavation and research 1978-1998*, vol. 1 'The surveys' (Stafford Borough Council, 2021). [History: Deborah Youngs, Philip Morgan, John Darlington and David Wilkinson; Earthwork and architectural survey: Marcus Jecock and Gary Corbett; Geophysical survey: John Darlington and Dan Sheil]
Drake, Maurice, *The Costessy Collection of Stained Glass* (1920)
Dugdale, Sir William, *Monasticon Anglicanum* (1655-73; Revised edition 1718)
Dugdale, Sir William, *The Baronage of England*, III (1675-6)
Egerton Castle (Ed.), *Jerningham Letters 1780-1843*, 2 vols. (London, 1896)
Ellis, R., *History of Thornbury Castle* (1839)
Green, M.A.E. (Ed.), *Calendar of the Proceedings of the Committee for the Advance of Money 1642-56*
Harris, B.J., *Edward Stafford 3rd Duke of Buckingham 1478-1521* (Stanford University Press, 1986)
Hawkyard, A.D.K., 'Some late medieval fortified manor houses: a study of the building works of Sir John Falstof, Ralph lord Cromwell and Edward Stafford, 3rd Duke of Buckingham.' (M.A. Keele, 1969)

Hervey, Mary, *Thomas Howard Earl of Arundel* (Cambridge University Press, 1921)

Hill, C., *Stafford Castle: interim reports* (Stafford Borough Council) 1980-1982. [1st report n.d.; 2nd (1980), 3rd (1981), 4th (1982)]

Historical Manuscripts Commission X Report iv, 55, Receivers Account for Dover

Howard, David, *Lord Arundel and His Circle* (1985)

Howard, Henry, *Memorials of the Howard Family* (1834)

Husenbeth, Revd R.C., *Discourse Pronounced at the Funeral of Frances Xavaria, Baroness Stafford*, 27 November 1832

Jerningham, H.E., *Reminiscences of an Attaché* (1886)

Johnes, Thomas (Ed.), *Sir John Froissart's Chronicles* (1802)

Langdale, Hon. Charles, *Memoirs of Mrs Fitzherbert* (1856)

Levine, M., 'The Fall of the Duke of Buckingham', *Tudor Men and Institutions* (Louisiana, 1972)

Leslie, Anita, *Mrs Fitzherbert* (Hutchinson, 1960)

Leslie, Shane, *Mrs Fitzherbert* (Burns Oates and Washburne)

McFarlane, K.B., *The Nobility of Later Medieval England* (O.U.P., 1973). ('The Beauchamps and the Staffords', pp.187-212)

Munson, Jeremy, *Maria Fitzherbert, The Secret Wife of George IV* (Constable, 2001)

Norgate, T.B., *History of Costessy* (1972)

Paston Letters I, 61; I, 355-7; I, 407-9

Rawcliffe, Carole, *The Staffords, Earls of Stafford and Dukes of Buckingham 1394-1521* (Cambridge University Press, 1978)

Rawcliffe, Carole, 'The Staffords, Earls of Stafford and Dukes of Buckingham' (Ph.D. Sheffield, 1974)

Robinson, J.M., *The Dukes of Norfolk* (O.U.P., 1982)

Rot Parl V. 206

Rowney, I.D., 'The Staffordshire political community, 1440-1500' (Ph.D. Keele, 1981)

Skinner, David, 'Nicholas Ludford ... with a study of the Collegiate Chapel of the Holy Trinity, Arundel ...', (D. Phil. Thesis, Oxford, 1997)

Stafford's Memoires: Or a Brief and Impartial Account of the Birth and Quality, Imprisonment, Tryal, Principles, Declaration, Comportment, Devotion, Last Speech and Final End of William, late Viscount Stafford (1681)

Stafford Castle: A Brief History (Stafford Borough Council, 1988, reprinted 2001)

Stafford Castle: the Third Interim Report (Stafford Borough Council 1981). [Includes biographical notes on Ralph de Stafford (1299-1372).]

Stafford Castle (Staffordshire C.C. Education Department, 1969, revised 1979) [Stafford Castle 1160-1951. Readings from primary sources]

Stevenson, *Wars of England in France* I, II

Stubbs, William, *Constitutional History* (1900) III

Swinnerton, B.T. (Ed.), *Staffordshire Castles: a liberal studies handbook* (Stafford College of Further Education, 1971)

Turnbull, W.B.D.D. (Ed.), *Compota domestica familiarum de Buckingham et d'Angouleme* (Roxburghe Club, Edinburgh, 1836) [Includes household book for Humphrey, Duke of Buckingham, 1443-4.]

Turpyn, Richard, *Chronicle of Calais*, Henry VI Anno 21-Anno 29 (Camden Society, 1861)

V.C.H. *Staffordshire*, V, 82-4

V.C.H. *Shropshire*, I, 404

V.C.H. *Shropshire*, XI (1985) Telford

Wainright, Clive, *The Romantic Interior* (1989), 284

Walpole Society 26 (1937-8) 25-7; 'Vertue Notebooks' V

Wood Green, M.A.E., *Letters of Royal and Illustrious Ladies of Great Britain* (1846) II, 189

William Salt Library: Eyton, *Historical Collections Staffs.*, II pt. 1

Young, D. and Morgan, P., *Stafford Castle Archive and historical survey 1071-1653* (Keele, 1988)

The Speech of Wil. Howard Lord Viscount Stafford ... on Wednesday December 29 1680 (Printed for J. Clarke, Smithfield)

The Execution of the Popish Lord ... or, the Traytor's Downfall (December 1680)

A Catalogue of the Pictures, Prints, Drawings etc being part of the old Arundel Collection and belonging to the Late Earl of Stafford (1720)

ARTICLES/JOURNALS

Camden Society, II, 138, 'Wriothesley's Chronicle'

Compton-Reeves, A., 'Some of Humphrey Stafford's indentured retainers', *Nottingham Medieval Studies* xvi (1972), 80-91

Cantor, L.M., 'The medieval castles of Staffordshire', *N.S.J.F.S.* vi (1966), 38-46

de Mazzhingi, T.J., 'History of Castle Church', *Staff. Hist Coll.* VII (II) (1887), 1-152

Frith, J.B., 'A great medieval landlord', *Trans. Old Stafford Society* (1929), 21-37

Gage, J. (Ed.), 'Extracts from the Household Book of Edward Duke of Buckingham 1508-9', *Archaeologia*, xxv (1834), 311

Gage, J., *History and Antiquities of Hengrave* (1827)

Gentleman's Magazine, LXXVI pt. ii; CIII pt. I, 534

Gunton, Harry E., 'Costessey Brickworks', *Trans. Newcomen Soc.* (1968) XL, 165-8

Harris, B.J., 'Marriage sixteenth-century style: Elizabeth Stafford and the third duke of Norfolk', *Journal of Social History* xv (1981-2), 371-82

Harris, M. (Ed.), 'The account of the Great Household of Humphrey, first duke of Buckingham, for the year 1452-3', *Camden Misc.*, xxviii, Camden Soc., serv.4 xxix (1984), 1-57 [Introduction by J.M. Thurgood]

Langston, J.N., 'The Staffords of Thornbury Castle', *Bristol and Gloucester Archaeological Society*, 72 (1953), 83

Langston, J.N., 'Old catholic families of Gloucestershire: II The Staffords and Howards of Thornbury', *Trans. Bristol and Gloucester Arch. Soc.*, lxxii (1953), 79-104, plus genealogy

Mazzinghi, T.J., 'Castle Church', *William Salt Archaeological Soc*, viii (1887), 72-9

McKinley, R.A., 'The building of Stafford Castle', *Trans. Old Stafford Soc* (1959-63), 25 [Translation of building contract of 1348]

Morgan, P., 'The Domesday castles of Staffordshire', *Staffs Hist* v (1987), 42-8

Musset, L., 'Aux origines d'une class dirigeante: les Tosney, grands barons normands, du Xe au XIIIe siècle', *Francia* v (1977), 45-80

Neale, J.E., 'The fame of Sir Edward Stafford', *English Historical Review* XLIV (1929), 203-20

Palliser, D.M., 'The Castles at Stafford', *Stafford Historical and Civic Society* (1971-3), 1-17 [For an alternative history of Stafford Castle.]

Pugh, T.B., '"The indenture for the Marches" between Henry VII and Edward Stafford (1477-1521), Duke of Buckingham', *Eng. Hist. Review* lxxi (1956), 436-41

Rawcliffe, C., 'The papers of Edward, duke of Buckingham', *Journal of the Soc. of Archivists*, v (1976), 294-300

Read, Conyers, 'The fame of Sir Edward Stafford', *American Historical Review* XX (1915), 292-315

Read, Conyers, 'The fame of Sir Edward Stafford', *American Historical Review* XXV (1915), 560-6

Seguin, Colleen Marie, 'Addicted Unto Piety: Catholic Women in England 1590-1690', (Dissertation, Duke University, 1997)

Victorian Society Annual, 'Costessey brickworks' (1997), 26-7

Walpole Soc., 26 (1937-38), 'Vertue Notebooks Vol V'

Wrottesley, G., 'An account of the military service performed by Staffordshire tenants in the thirteenth and fourteenth centuries', *S.H.C.* viii pt. 1, 1-122

Wrottesley, G., 'Military service performed by Staffordshire tenants during the reign of Richard II', *S.H.C.* xiv, pt. 1, 221-64

Index

༄·ༀ

Page numbers in **bold** type refer to illustrations

abbeys: Conches (Normandy), 3; Evesham, 3; Tewkesbury, 39

Act of Uniformity, 52

Archbishops of Canterbury: Cardinal Reginald Pole, 52, 53; John Stafford, 14, 27

arms, **4**, **50**

Arundel, Earls of: 14th Earl (Thomas Howard), 58-60, 63, 129; 15th Earl (Henry Frederick Howard), 61, 66

Arundel (Stafford) Collection, xiii, 59-61, 67, 68, 77

Arundel House, 63, 67

Audley, Margaret (wife of Ralph 1st Earl), 7, 38, 128

Austin Friars, 12, 48

Bagot: Hervey, xii, 4, 128; Richard, 55-7

Bannister, Ralph, 33

Barcestre, John de, 10

Basset, Margaret (wife of Baron Edmund), 6, 18

Basset, Ralph (1st Earl), xii, 6, 7, **8**, 9, 128

Basset, Ralph, 16

battles: Bosworth, 34; Crecy, xii, 10; Flodden, 43; Northampton, xiii, 30; St Albans, 28-9; Shrewsbury, 18; Therouanne (1513), 43

Beaufort, Cardinal, 22, 23, 27

Beaufort, Margaret (wife of Humphrey Earl of Stafford), 27, 29, 30, 37, 128

Bedingfield, Sir Henry, 102, 107

Bishop of Exeter, Edmund, 12-14

Bohun, Eleanor de, 17, 18, 32

Bolton Row, 89, 106

Bonaparte, Napoleon, 92, 107, 108

Bourchiers, the, 21, 22, 26, 27, 29, 30

Bradley (Castle Church), 1, 2, 3

Bramshall, 4

Brown, John, 94

Buckingham, Dukes of: 1st Duke (Humphrey), xii, 19-30, 128; 2nd Duke (Henry), xiii, 30-33, 128; 3rd Duke (Edward), xiii, 34-49, 128

Buckingham, Earls of, 17, 19, 26

Buckler, John Chessel, 100-102, 108-9

Burghley, Lord, viii, 54

Burnet, Bishop, 69, 71

Burney, Fanny, 86-7

Butler Bowden chasuble, **20**, 28

Byron, Lord, 87

Calais, Captain of, 23-5

Caroline, Queen, 121

cartularies, 50

castles: Arundel, 59, 63, 78; Bohun, 18; Brecon, 36; Caus, 8, 52; Deresloyn, 6; Dover, **25**; Gloucester, 45; Maxstoke, 28, 37; Scarborough, 53; Stafford, xi, xii, xiii, xiv, 2, 3, 4, **5**, 10, **13**, 37-8, 49, 50, 52, 55, 62-3, 67, 78, 94-5, 110; Thornbury, xii, xiii, 35, 37, 38-9, 42, 47, 49, 78, 102; Tonbridge, xii, 12, 37, 45

Catholic Emancipation, xiv, 89, 96, 98, 107

Charles I, 57

Charles II, 60, 68

Chesterfield, Lord, 82, 85

Civil War, viii, 52, 62, 125

Clare, Gilbert de, 7, 32
Clarence, Duke of, 12
Claude Charlotte (wife of 1st Earl), 76, 129
Commonwealth, 65, 68
Corbet, Alice, 8
Constable of Dover Castle and Warden of the
    Cinque Ports, 24-6, 31
Costessey, xiv, 78, 79, 80, **81**, 85, 87, 89, 90, 91,
    95, 98-106, 107, 108-9, 126
Cromwell, Thomas, 50
Croydon Palace, 14, 15

Delabeare, Sir Richard, 35-6
Dellacourt, Edmund, 45, 47
Derby, Earls of, vii, 9, 11, 125
Devonshire, Duchess of, 113-15
Dillon, Frances *see* Jerningham, Lady
Dissolution of Monasteries, 50
Domesday Book, 2, 4
Dugdale, Stephen, 70, 71

Earl of Mercia, 3
Edmund, Baron de Stafford, 6, 128
Edmund 5th Earl of Stafford, xii, 16, 128
Edward I, 4, 6
Edward II, 6
Edward III, 7, 9, 10, 11, 12, 48
Edward IV (Duke of York), 26, 28, 29, 30
Edward V, 32, 33
Edward VI, 49, 50
Edward VII (Prince of Wales), 109
Edwin, Earl, 1
Eglinton Tournament, 110, 111
Elizabeth, Queen, 52, 53, 55
Erasmus, 50, 52
Evelyn, John, 66, 69, 70, 71
Ewens, Elizabeth (Countess of Stafford), **77**

Flanders, 63, 64, 65, 68, 75, 92
Fox, Charles James, 113, 116, 119
France, 39, 43, 45, 53, 55, 56, 65, 77, 82, 83, 84,
    85, 89, 94, 107, 111-12
French Revolution, 81, 90-2, 120
Fitzherberts (*see also* Stafford, Lord), vii, 68; Sir
    Anthony, viii, 125, 129; Basil of Norbury, 125;
    Basil Thomas, xiv, 110, 111, 124, 130; Francis,

110; Mrs (Maria Smythe), viii-ix, xiv, 110, 111-
    24, 125; John, vii-viii, 129; Sir John, vii, 129;
    Thomas, viii, 111-13, 125, 126; Thomas of
    Swynnerton, 125; Sir Thomas, viii, 129;
    William, vii, 125; William of Somersall, 125

George III, 82, 92, 107, 120
George IV (Prince of Wales), ix, 86, 96, 98, 107,
    110, 113-23
Gilbert, Robert, 45, 47
Gillray, James, 119
Gloucester, Dukes of, 16, 17, 19, 25, 48, 107
Gloucestershire holdings, 49, 52
Gordon Riots, 111

Hampshire holdings, 32
Hastang, Katherine (wife of Ralph 2nd Earl), 7,
    128
Hastings, Sir Hugh, 8
Henry I, 2
Henry II, 3
Henry IV, 13, 17
Henry V, 18, 21
Henry VI, 21, 22, 27, 28, 29, 30
Henry VII, 33, 34, 36, 37, 42, 59
Henry VIII, viii, xi, 37, 43, 44-5, 46, 49, 50, 59
Holland, 66, 68
Holman, Ann (Countess of Stafford), **76**, 129
Holy Roman Emperor, 65
Household Book, 50, **51**
Howard, Philip (Cardinal Norfolk), 69
Hugh 2nd Earl of Stafford, xii, 11, 14, 16, 28, 128
Humphrey, Earl of Stafford, 27, 29, 128
Hundred Years War, xi, xii, 7, 9-12, 14-16, 21-3

Italy, 65, 67, 69

James I, 59, 80
James II, 69, 75, 76
Jerninghams (*see also* Stafford, Lord), vii, xiv, 64,
    65, 68, 79-111; Charles 'the Chevalier', 82, 83,
    85, 91, 130; Charlotte (Bedingfield), 85, 86, 87-
    8, 93, 94, 97, 106, 130; Edward, 88-9, 92, **93**,
    94-6, 97-8, 107, 130; Edward Stafford, 110,
    111, 123-4, 130; Edward 'the Poet', 82, 85-7,

92, 107, 130; Emily Charlotte, xiv, 110, 124-5, 130; George Sulyard Stafford, 108; Sir Henry, 79; Sir Hubert Edward Henry, 107-8, 130; William, 88-9, 92, 130

Jerningham, Lady (Frances Dillon), 83, 84, 85, 87, 88, 89, 91, 92, 97, 106, 107, 111, 117, 120, 130; (Mary Plowden), 78, 82, 85, 130; (Frances Sulyard), 94, **99**, 100, 106, 130

Jersey, Lady, 120-1

Joan of Arc, 27

Kent holdings, 12, 17, 25, 35

Knot, 14, **24**, 27-8, 38, 39, 109

Knyvett, Charles, 45, 47

Liddell, Annie, 108, 130

Lord Chancellor, 13, 14

Lord High Constableship, xiii, 31, 33, 34, 43, 45, 49

Lord Lieutenant of Staffordshire, 50, 52

Lords of Stafford, 3

Louis XV, 89, 108, 112

Louis XVIII, 107, 122

Lucas, Sir Thomas, 46-7

Magdalene College, Cambridge, 35, **46**

Mary, Queen, 49, 52, 53, 59, 79, **82**

Mary Queen of Scots, 54

Millicent (d. of Robert of Stafford), 4, 128

Montevile (Montville), 2

More, Thomas, viii, 33, 47

Napoleon III, Emperor, 107

Nevill, Lady Anne (wife of 1st Duke of Buckingham), 19, 32, 128

Newport holdings, 7, 17

Norbury, Derbys., vii, viii, 125

Norfolk, Dukes of, xiii, 35, 43, 44, 47; 5th Duke, 59, 64; 6th Duke (Lord Henry), 60, 66, 67-8; 8th Duke, 78; 11th Duke, 84, 97-8; 12th Duke, 96, 98

Norfolk holdings, 6, 47

Northumberland, Duke of, 49

Oates, Titus, xiv, 70-1

Pantulf, William, 2

Paston Letters, 28

Penshurst Place, 26, 37, 43, 44

Percy, Alianora (wife of 3rd Duke of Buckingham), 43, 49, 128

Pitt, William, 87, 97

Plantaganet, Lady Anne (wife of Edmund 5th Earl), 16-17, 19, 31, 128

Plowden, Mary *see* Jerningham, Lady

Poland, 53

Pole, Cardinal Reginald, 52, 53

Pole, Ursula (wife of 1st Baron), 44, 52, 129

priories: Kenilworth, 3; Stone, 3, 4, 6, 12, 16; Wootton Wawen, 3

religion, vii, viii, xii, 27, 39-40, 50-1, 63-5, 79, 92

Richard II, 13, 16

Richard III, xiii, 31, 32-4, 47, 59

Robert de Toeni (of Stafford), xii, 1-3, 128

Rupert, Prince of the Rhine, 62

Russell, John, 45

St George, John, 45

St George's Chapel, Windsor, 39, 48

St John's Hospital, 12

Seneschal: of Aquitaine, 9; of Gascony, 12

Seymour, Minnie, 122

Shakespeare, William, 47

Sheriff of Staffordshire, 3

Shifnal Estate, xiii-xiv, **64**, 68, 78, 90, 100, 110

Smythe, Marianne, ix, xiv, 110, 111, 122-4, 130

Soane, Sir John, 89

Somerset, Duke of, 29, 50-1

Spanish Armada, viii, 55

Stafford burgh, 1,2

Stafford, Sir Edward, 54-5, 129; Sir Richard, 12, 128; Roger, 57, 129; Thomas, 52-3; William, 53-4

Stafford, Countess of (Ann Holman), 76, 129; (Elizabeth Ewens), **77**; (Mary Stafford), xiii-xiv, 57-60, 62-3, 65-6, 69, 75, **76**, 97, 129

Stafford, Earls of, 4, 11, 16, 18: 1st Earl (Henry), 75-6, 129; 2nd Earl (William), 76-8, 79, 129; 3rd Earl (William Matthias), 77-8, 79, 129; 4th Earl (John Paul), xiv, **77**, 78, 81, 129

Stafford, Lady Catherine, **22**; Lady Elizabeth (d. of 3rd Duke of Buckingham), 44, 50, 59; Lady

Isobel (Forster), 62

Stafford, Lord, 6; 1st Baron (Henry Howard), xi, xiii, 44, 45, 49-52, 53, 129; 2nd Baron (Henry), 50, 52, 129; 3rd Baron (Edward), xiii, 52, 53, 55-6, 129; 4th Baron (Edward), 52, 56, 63, 129; 5th Baron (Henry), xiii, 52, 57, 129; 6th Baron (Sir George Jerningham), 78, 82, **83**, 85, 129, 130; 7th Baron (Sir William), 82-3, 84, 88, 89-90, 91-2, 93, 94, 95-6, 97-8, 107, 130; 8th Baron (George), xiv, 88-9, 94, **95**, 97-100, 107, 110, 130; 9th Baron (Henry Valentine Stafford), 108-9, 130; 10th Baron (Augustus), 109, 123, 130; 11th Baron (Fitzherbert), 109, 123, 130; 11th Baronet (Henry), 109, 130; 12th Baron (Francis Edward Fitzherbert), xiv, 124, 126-7, 130; 13th Baron (Edward), **126**, 127, 130; 14th Baron (Basil), 127, 130; 15th Baron (Francis), xi, 127, 130

Stafford, Nicholas de, 3, 6, 128

Stafford, Robert of, 3

Stafford, Viscount, William Howard, xiii-xiv, 57-63, 65-6, 67-75, 78, 97, 98

Stafford Howard, Aletheia, 63, **74**; Lady Anastasia, 71, 76, 81, 89, 91, 96, 97, 129; Francis, 74; Isabella, 71, **73**; John, **74**, 77, 78, 129; Louisa, 77; Lady Mary, 63, 87-8; Lady Ursula, 69; Xaveria, 77

Stafford Prayer Book, **41**, 42

Staffordshire holdings, xi, 3, 49

Stanhope, Lady Hester, 112, 119

Steward of the King's Household, 8

Sulyard, Frances *see* Jerningham, Lady

Surrey, Earl of, Henry Howard, 58

Sussex, Duke of, **99**

Swynnerton, vii, viii, 89, 110, 125-7

Tart Hall (Stafford House), xiii-xiv, 61, 67, 68, 77

Test Act, 70

Thornbury College, 39, 40

Thomas 3rd Earl of Stafford, 16, 128

Treaty of Bretigny, 12

Tutbury, Prior of, vii, 125

Victoria, Queen, 124

Wake, Joan (wife of Hugh 2nd Earl), 28

Wales holdings, 18, 32, 37, 46

Walpole, Horace, 82, 85

Walsingham, Sir Francis, 54-5

Wars of the Roses, 27-34

Warwick, Duke of, 26

Warwick, Earls of, 10, 11, 23, 30

Welsh Marches, xi, xiii, 8-9, 17, 35, 46, 47, 49

West Indies, 107-8

William IV, 106, 124

William 4th Earl of Stafford, 16, 128

William the Conqueror, xii, 1, 2, 3

Wolsey, Cardinal, 43, 45, 47

Woodville (Wydvill), Katherine (wife of 2nd Duke of Buckingham), 30, 128

Wynkyn de Worde, 42

Yorkshire holdings, 17, 32, 35